Evangelism's Open Secrets

Herb Miller

C B P Press
St. Louis, Missouri

Third printing, 1988

Library of Congress Cataloging in Publication Date

Miller, Herb.
  Evangelism's open secrets.
  1. Evangelistic work. 2. Church Work. I. Title.
BV3790.M6   254.5   77-23468

ISBN: 0-8292-0805-7

Distributed in Canada by The G. R. Welch Company, Ltd., Toronto, Ontario, Canada

Printed in the United States of America

Dedication

To Barbara, who patiently raised a family while I went fishing.

Acknowledgements

Many pastors opened their doors and minds to make this inquiry possible. I am grateful for their kindly cooperation in making their successful ideas available to other fishermen. Thanks also to Harry Bridwell, a seasoned angler whose statistical research and thought sharpening mind brought the ideas to a focus.

Contents

INTRODUCTION

Framing the Picture

"Our church is really starting to grow," Harry said proudly. "We had three additions yesterday. Four came in the Sunday before that."

"That sounds great. Tell me, what are you doing to make that happen?" replied John as he wheeled the small foreign car onto the interstate ramp.

As the two pastors rode toward a committee meeting at the synod office downstate, Harry enlarged on his leadership feats. John continued to mumble appropriate approbations. How exhilarating it must be to pastor such a church, he thought. I wonder why that isn't happening in our congregation?

Later that month, John was gathering statistical figures for a congregational business meeting report. He was hoping to raise the sights of the board members concerning their evangelism responsibility. Flipping through the annual yearbook of his denomination, his eye stumbled over a line close below his own church. It showed the figures for Harry's congregation. Curious, he extracted the membership totals for the last few years and placed them beside his own. The numbers were startling. Harry's church showed almost no net growth. In fact, during the past three years their active membership had increased by only eight people.

Such verbal overkills are one of the biggest reasons why church persons turn blank ears toward new evangelism methods, or even make fun of them. Churchly meetings are always filled with solid sounding theories. But honest examinations of parish head counts often reveal track records unequal to idea records. How difficult it is to divide success stories from ego smog.

These delusions of grandeur even brainwash denomination executives. One poll of such leaders asked for a list of congregations within their jurisdiction which were showing rapid growth. Replies were then checked against factual figures in the denomination's yearbook. Less than 20 percent had an accurate perception of which churches were growing. Pastors who talk effusively about their successes evidently achieve a fairly high rate of believers, even among hardheaded administrators. The myth is not dead. It is alive and well in American churchmen.

Using a reverse investigation approach, membership figures of 482 congregations of the Christian Church (Disciples of Christ) were analyzed during a five year period. Most were in the Southwest; some were from other parts of the country. Records were taken from denominational yearbooks rather than word-of-mouth "guesstimates." Those congregations with "consistent growth" were then studied at close range. Using open-ended interview techniques, a search was conducted for the practical principles which might lie behind the growth figures. As well as talking with pastors, many laypersons were interviewed separately. The following chapters are a transcript of evidence gleaned in those probes.

What is meant by the term "consistently growing?" Not just churches with big baptism figures each year. A congregation (especially large ones) can show gigantic annual baptism totals and a simultaneous decline in net membership. In some large city churches, Sunday morning invitation hymns always pull in several fish. But more folks may be moving out of town, transferring to other churches, and dying each week than are being baptized. Thus, like a well-groomed corpse, a congregation can have the appearance of vitality while traveling toward the numerical cemetery.

Similarly, many churches add large numbers of members by transfer each year. But this doesn't always mean the church is growing. More often it means they are surviving. Sometimes it doesn't even mean that. If you project their past five years of net decline for twenty years into the future, the result is often a disaster chart.

"Consistent growth" as used here describes a congregation averaging at least 10 percent per year net growth in active membership during the last five years. To put it another way, a church which has grown 50 percent in total active membership over a five year period has averaged 10 percent net growth each year.

Of the 482 churches analyzed, 68 percent had declined in net active membership during the five year period. But thirty congregations qualified for the five year-50 percent net growth category. This destroys another myth—the commonly held belief that no churches anywhere are growing in these difficult times. Some churches are growing—many at a rate far above the 50 percent-five year figure. One church grew 307 percent. Twelve others grew more than 100 percent (more than doubled in size) during the five year span.

Nor is there any correlation between community population growth and church growth. Some of these thirty growing churches are in counties with rapidly growing population; others are in counties with a slight decline in population. Even if the congregation is situated in a growing population pool, it is often the only growing church for miles around. Other congregations in the same pool may be standing still or declining. Some of the growing congregations are young (less than ten years); some are more than a hundred years old. Some are liberal in theology; some are conservative. Some are in large cities like Houston; others are in small towns. Some are served by ministers under thirty years old; one by a man of fifty-five.

No attempt was made to measure spiritual depth of the members in these churches. Only God can determine that. Nor was there an effort to judge the level of Christian commitment in new persons joining the growing congregations. That, too, is best left to God, who alone knows what lies beneath exterior decisions. But some things can be said with objective assurance concerning the churches studied. At least ten percent more people are forming a previously unformed affiliation with these branch offices of Christ's church each year than are moving away, dying, or becoming inactive.

"Have you done any research in the churches that aren't growing?" asked a layman during an interview.

"Very little," was the reply. Whatever positive things growing congregations are doing, it is assumed that non-growing ones lack these traits. If you wish to find out what makes a church grow, you don't ask someone whose church isn't. He either doesn't know how or isn't applying what he does know.

"But perhaps the congregation's environmental situation prevents growth from occuring," the man persisted.

In a few cases that may be factual, but such defenses are at best irrelevant to the art-science of evangelism and at worst a cop-out for lazy brain cells. They may even be demonic. Can you imagine Paul comforting the churches in Asia Minor with that kind of terminology?

Evangelism is defined herein as the winning of the allegiance of *new* persons to the Lordship of Jesus Christ. Many will disagree with that and wish to define it another way. They may feel that evangelism also takes place with persons who are already members. "The church is not as much a force for evangelism as it is a field for evangelism," one man said.

There is truth in that kind of definition, but limited truth. It smudges evangelism to the point where we stop distinguishing between *growth in Christ*—also an authentic New Testament

9

task—and *winning new persons to Christ* (persons previously unaffiliated with his church in any way). The whole truth involves the necessity to do both; win new persons to Christ initially, and then continually help them mature after they make that basic decision.

But let the reader beware that our purpose here is to uncover factors that produce new birth in Christ, not the factors which encourage Christian maturity after that birth occurs. To lump these in two separate camps is admittedly false dichotomizing. They do overlap at many points. Good nutrition produces both healthy babies and healthy growth following birth. And the factors that encourage new birth in Christ can also promote postnatal maturity in those same new Christians. But reviewing the overlaps is not our concern here. Rather, we are seeking to isolate the principles that could appropriately be listed under a column headed "Christian Obstetrical Procedures."

Part I
Demythologizing Church Growth

1
THREE GOLDEN THREADS

"What we need is a good pulpit man. People won't come if you bore them limp."

"Let's get serious about our community's social action needs. Then people will be interested in joining our church. Pie-in-the-sky talk just isn't enough anymore."

"Start a Sunday church school attendance campaign and church membership will come up. When the kids don't come, parents won't either, you know."

"If we had a good youth program, this church might grow. Why, I remember when. . . ."

"I wish our preacher would get out of his office and call on people. That's what folks really want, something personal. You have to mix with people."

Sound plausible, don't they? Yet many nongrowing churches are

11

served by truly great pulpit men. And we can all name strong youth programs in numerically calcified congregations. Ibid, ibid, ibid, through all the other magic prescriptions. If none of these is the Salk vaccine for statistical paralysis, what does produce growth in a church?

Before we can hear the real answer to that question, we must get a cure for the secondary disease that complicates our case—"Oversimplificationitis." This malady creates the mental delusion that church growth is caused by a single ingredient. Not so. Consistent growth is rarely the result of waving one magic wand over present programming.

A motor drives a car by careful integration of many component parts. Cylinders turn over at appropriate times. The carburetor supplies fuel in the right air-to-gasoline ratio. The battery sends electric spark to clean plugs. Subtract any one of these and even a Mercedes stands stationary in the garage. Similarly, church growth comes from a combination of factors, each worthless without the others.

What are these ingredients? The number is endless if you count all the subtechniques. That would be like trying to total all the nuts and bolts in an engine. But limit yourself to major causes and there are only three: (1) Being the Word—the influence of the Christian's spiritual quality and example. (2) Doing the Word—the influence of the Christian's loving acts toward other people. (3) Saying the Word—the influence of the Christian's verbal communication with those outside the church. Each factor is equal in value; none is superior to the others. Nor is there any significance in the order of their listing. None is necessarily an outgrowth of doing one or both of the others. You can start with any of the three, as long as you eventually do them all. If you don't, consistent growth will not happen.

Casting the trilogy into a mathematical equation, we would put it this way: A strong emphasis on the spiritual renewal disciplines like prayer and Bible study, plus a strong emphasis on performing unselfish loving acts toward fellow human beings, plus a strong emphasis on some form of verbal communication with those outside the church, equals congregational growth.

This equation is timeless and universal. It applies to churches of all size, location, ethnic group, racial mix, or theological perspective. Look at John Wesley's Methodist movement: (1) strong personal relationship with God through spiritual disciplines; (2) great love and compassion for others, especially the poverty-stricken working class; (3) every convert an active evangelist verbalizing the faith to others. Check the formula against the radical, but rapidly growing, Jehovah's Witness movement today. Same factors. Scratch below the peel of every consistently growing congregation and you will discover a similar pattern.

Jesus so saturated his ministry with these three points that they're

12

easily overlooked. "You shall love the Lord your God with all your heart, and with all your soul, and with all your mind. This is the great and first commandment. And a second is like it, You shall love your neighbor as yourself." (Matt. 22:37-39) "Go therefore and make disciples of all nations. . . ." (Matt. 28:19) And he sent out the seventy to do just that. The early church took these three principles and exploded with vitality across a decaying Roman Empire.

Can you erase one factor from the formula and still have a church? Yes, just as you still have a motor when you disconnect the battery. But you won't have much growth. Look at some of the evangelism systems of the 1950s that got such big gains in only a few months. One of the three basics was present—"Saying the Word" by the technique of calling on prospects. And that produces results, at least temporarily. But one or both of the other two components was often absent. Leaders lacked the methods, or the inclination, to encourage their additions in spiritual growth. So they soon converted to subtractions. Or, the new members were not quickly involved in unselfish Christian service. So they fell away as fast as they had fallen toward. Unfortunately, even the leaders in these programs seldom understood exactly what had caused their success, or their subsequent failure.

Our blindness to this three-pronged equation is increased by growing churches themselves. They often can't see the equation either, even though they participate in it. When asked for their secret of success, they frequently give credit to some subtechnique within one of the big three. The evangelistic truth seeker is thus given more false proof for his "oversimplificationitis." And because he is so convinced that growth can come from only one-third of the formula (or some supporting fraction of the one-third), he is mentally blocked from learning the broader truth.

For example, let's take a look at a congregation which appears to be growing because of a strong emphasis on "Being the Word."

	1970-71	1976	% Change
Active Membership—[1]	66	180	+172.7%
Inactive Membership—	7	9	+ 28.5%
Annual Budget—	$9,718	$40,875	+320.6%
Annual Missions Giving—	$ 835	$ 1,775	+112.6%
	1970	1974	
County Population—[2]	2,918	8,700	+198.1%

Born in 1955, the congregation added a new sanctuary one year ago. The worship service is already using the overflow room, and leaders are pondering the need for another new building. The fourteen other churches in the community are achieving little or no growth. Staff consists of the thirty-six year old pastor, who has served the church for seven years, plus a full-time office secretary added during the last two years. This is a resort community.[3]

In all the personal interviews with members and pastor, the most prominent reason for growth is the strong teaching and preaching emphasis on a personal relationship with God. This church has not grown in response to a specific promotional program or plan. There was no membership campaign, no systematic visitation program, no goal-setting by the church board or congregation. The growth appears spontaneous. New members seem to have responded to what the church is—it seems to meet their needs, so they join it.

But then five hours of tape-recorded interviews with the pastor and laypersons were dissected in a careful search into reasons everyone had said were contributing to the rapid growth. The following is a summary of that list:

1. Planning programs to glorify God
2. Faith in God's help and leadership
3. Bible-centered study
4. "Praising God Moments" in worship services
5. Preaching—biblical, non-judgmental, optimistic, forgiving, spiritual emphasis, relaxed
6. Programming to meet human need of various community age groups
7. Nondoctrinal approach
8. Relaxed atmosphere of the church
9. Lack of conflict within the congregation
10. Acceptance by members and pastor of all kinds of people— good and bad, rich and poor
11. Friendliness of laypersons
12. Good fellowship events meeting various needs of various age groups in the church
13. Strong youth work programming
14. Good summer youth program for all ages
15. People wanting to share their enjoyment with others
16. Enthusiasm
17. Many contacts by members of the church with prospects
18. Good pastoral leadership
19. Much pastoral calling on members and newcomers
20. Minister's ability to relate to people on a personal basis
21. Church leadership aggressively seeking new ideas and growth
22. Involving new members quickly into the church decision-making structure
23. Laypersons responsible for and involved in programs
24. Community population growth

Now look at the list again. All three golden threads—doing the Word, saying the Word, and being the Word—are readily apparent.

Another congregation appears to be achieving rapid growth through a strong emphasis on "Doing the Word."

14

	Five Years Ago	At Present	% Change
Active Membership—	370	753	+103.5%
Inactive Membership—	95	200	+110.5%
Annual Budget—	$70,544	$140,754	+ 99.5%
Annual Missions Giving—	$18,928	$ 26,853	+ 41.9%

Located in a large growing metropolitan area, this congregation was born fifteen years ago. The present pastor, age forty-nine, has served them twelve years. An associate minister was added three years ago. More recently, a licensed layman has been employed to do hospital calling.[4]

The most obvious trait noted by the casual onlooker would be the strong emphasis on service. Every kind of activity is invited into the building, from boy scout troups and girl scout troups to a day school with one hundred children and thirteen teachers every day. Used as a precinct voting place, it hosts hospital meetings when that facility is short of space. Spillovers are taken from everywhere in the community, like group meetings for the development of a new community park. Haven for a widow's group, it also shelters sixty to eighty singles who call themselves "Persons Who Need Persons."

In reaching beyond the building, many members work at the hospital; several men visit the penitentiary; and the congregation supports a family counseling center. They are in the exploration stage of constructing a home for retarded adults. In summarizing their concern for others, the pastor says, "In everything we do, we seek to promote the awareness that being in society is being Christian. Jesus came to save this world and to show us how to live in this world, not the next one."

But a close examination also reveals the other two golden threads woven into the pattern. There is a strong emphasis on a dynamic and different kind of worship service. The pastor lists worship as the first of three reasons for the congregation's existence (along with education and service). Added to this is a large amount of contact with prospects. Laypeople go calling once a week. The pastor makes more than one hundred calls on members and prospects each month and insists on a like amount by every staff member. He has kept this pace for more than twelve years. "If you make ten calls a day in business, you'll make two sales," he says. "And the same is true of a church—of anything."

A third congregation seems to be growing as a result of "Saying the Word" in a systematic manner.

	Five Years Ago	At Present	% Change
Active Membership—	351	818	+133.0%
Inactive Membership—	134	155	+ 15.7%
Annual Budget—	$ 51,139	$114,601	+124.0%
Annual Missions Giving—	$ 12,319	$ 40,979	+232.6%
City Population—	359,700	360,411	+ .2%

15

This congregation was born in 1837. Four congregations of the same denomination within a six mile radius of the front door show inconsequential growth patterns over the same five year period. Staff consists of the pastor, a full-time Minister of Leadership Development added one year ago, a part-time music director-organist, and one full-time secretary. This is a suburban community.[5]

Suspects and prospects are gathered from many sources: (1) get-acquainted pads passed down the pew at worship services; (2) real estate transfers and marriage notices from the local newspaper (a ministry convalescent members render at home by reading the paper); (3) contacts which members encounter in the routine of business relationships; (4) new families who move into homes near those of present members; (5) the Welcome Wagon.

After the pastor obtains the name, he calls on the family. If they were in worship for the first time on Sunday, he *always* sees them the following week. If the name was obtained from another source, he introduces himself and tells them where he learned about them. In both cases, he talks to them about the denomination in general (if their own background is different) and tells them about his congregation specifically—its programs, ministries, services, and involvements.

During the conversation, he attempts to learn the names, ages and grades of their children, place of the adults' employment, their denominational background, former place of residence, and any related information which help in the cultivation process.

His visit seldom lasts more than fifteen to twenty minutes. In leaving, he drops the suggestion that as they look around for a church home they may find it helpful to try each church for a month at a time rather than jumping from church to church each Sunday. While he has suggested that they try *any* church for a month; if they follow his suggestion, they will probably try his first.

Returning to the office after such a call, he writes down all the pertinent information he has gleaned. The church secretary then types this information on a prepared letterhead which: (1) asks a person or family to make a call on the family this week, (2) gives some suggestions on how to make a call, (3) tells them what to do following the call, and (4) has a space on the back of the page for them to write their comments and feelings about their visit.

For the outside of the envelope, he dictates the names of four families whom he thinks would be "naturals" to call in this home. These may be people who live in the same area, work in similar professions, have children the same age, teach church school classes the age of some of the children, are from the same hometown, etc. Having such common denominators is a helpful entrée for both the caller and the called upon. Enclosed in the envelope are brochures which describe the congregation and denomination. Giving these to the family often provides helpful conversation starters as well as useful information.

16

The following Sunday morning, the evangelism chairman will give the envelope to one of the four names or families listed on the outside. The caller returns the envelope the following Sunday. Thus, four different laypersons visit in each prospect's home once per week during the following month. Some of the members prefer to call ahead before they visit; some don't. Letting the callers choose their own night seems to work better for this church than having a fixed calling night during each week. Telephoning rather than making a personal call is acceptable only if a visit is absolutely impossible.

During these visits, the couple, person, or youth simply give their reasons for choosing that church as their own church home. They talk about the programs, opportunities, and challenges the congregation offers. The value of the visit is thought to come not just from the content of what is shared, but from the spirit in which it is communicated—a personal witness about the congregation's positive aspects.

People moving into a new community may well expect the pastor to visit, and he usually does—maybe from several denominations. But when laypersons take time to make a call, that says to the family, "They must really care about me." When this happens four consecutive weeks by four different families, it makes a significant impression.

The pastor summarizes the calling this way, "There is nothing 'heavy' or theological about our calling. Verbalizing your faith experiences in a theological manner is difficult for some people, and sometimes frightening, both for the visitor and the visited. And isn't it a bit presumptuous to assume that a total stranger wants to know the intimate details of your personal migration of faith? But it is seldom inappropriate to assume they will want to hear how this congregation can minister to the needs of their family."

A month or six weeks after the pastor's first visit, providing the prospects have been attending and participating, he returns to make the "commitment call." He tells them that he has been happy to have them attending and asks if they have any questions, comments, or observations they would like to visit about.

They usually respond by telling him that several people from the church have visited them. How nice—and unusual—that has been! Other comments include: the friendliness of the people at your church, the programs they have become involved in, and the general atmosphere of the congregation.

During this commitment call—which is usually the sixth personal contact by someone from the church—he asks them about uniting with their fellowship *this* Sunday. And there is never a better time. For example: Fall is a good time because summer vacationing is over and new fall programs are underway; the Thanksgiving season is next, then Advent and Christmas; identifying with a new church home is an excellent way to begin a new year; then comes the Lent and Easter

17

season, the spiritual highlight of the Christian year; then we have Mother's Day, Childrens' Day, Father's Day. . . . In between, congregational dinners which recognize new members provide a good "due date." So every Sunday is an excellent time to unite with the church.

But the enormous value of this systematic plan for making large numbers of positive contacts can easily obscure the presence of the other two golden threads. The congregation is using an equally brilliant system for extending the love of God through the many laypersons who constantly help new members get acquainted and become involved.[6] And the quality of programming to meet spiritual, educational, service, and recreational needs for all age groups is equal to the "saying" and "doing" aspects of their congregational life.

2
TODAY'S INVISIBLE HERESIES

George Kinsey grew up in the dust bowl thirties of western Oklahoma. His church background was conservative, an ideology he never thought to question. During his last year of seminary Japanese planes bombed Pearl Harbor. Health preventing him from chaplaincy duty, he was soon serving an older congregation in a small town. There he ministered to self-sufficient ranchers and tradespeople. In their mind, religious training for children and dignified burial of parents and grandparents was a pastor's chief purpose. With the fading of the war, their greatest threat to a stable culture was too little rain for the wheat crop.

George soon developed great skill in pastoral care, though that term was not yet invented. His funeral sermons were described as comforting and eloquent. Easy to talk with, he was a good mixer and an excellent pulpit man. The call to a larger church in the next county soon rewarded his conscientious efforts.

In each new parish, George always intended to put a greater stress on evangelism. But there seemed little opportunity to practice his intentions. The people he served had already been exposed to a long series of persistent preachers. Occasionally some invitation-scarred veteran broke down and started coming to church. But George was never sure that this was a result of his evangelistic ability. Sometimes he suspected that the man was bored with life and had decided to try something new.

After twenty-five years, George thought he knew what made a church grow. You loved the people. You organized church suppers to which members could bring neighbors and friends. You called often in homes. You attended Lions Club meetings and responded with enthusiasm to every request for community service. You encouraged parishioners to invite people to church. You preached strong evangelistic messages, and about once a year you held a revival meeting. If you did this long enough, every once in a while someone would join the church.

When George heard stories of visitation campaigns used in suburban areas, he was amazed at the energy some ministers put into such projects. Just hearing a description of the whole complicated system made him tired. He wondered how they ever found time to get it done. He was also skeptical about the results. He knew it wouldn't work in his town.

John Polk graduated from seminary in 1951. A gifted preacher, he was a personable young man. Older clergymen described him as a comer in the ministry. Because of this reputation, he was picked by the bishop to pastor a new congregation on the edge of a large city.

John, and everyone else, assumed that growth would occur effortlessly. New neighborhoods were exploding like crabgrass in every direction. He would preach good sermons, launch a strong youth program, and enjoy a successful ministry. How glamorous this sounded. During student days in seminary he had served a conservative rural congregation. The prospect of dealing with more urbane, open-minded folks looked like freedom from prison.

Some of these expectations came true. People who spend early adult years moving around the country develop a pleasant flexibility of thinking. Open to new ideas, they are eager to organize a comprehensive church program. But other factors bloomed less happily. John soon discovered that about twenty percent of his members migrated away each year. On their way up the corporate ladder, or chasing other rainbows, they moved away even faster than housing developers could plant new concrete slabs. The sheer task of finding pew replacements became a weary load. Even more demanding was the job of replacing departing Sunday church school teachers. In one class he had recruited two new teachers during the last eight months. After adding

20

up the totals on his annual conference report at the end of the second year, John knew that something would have to be done.

That same month, he heard about a friend of his who had started a new kind of visitation program. The story said it was working in unbelievable proportions. The church had doubled in size after only six months. Desperate, he called his friend to see if they could have lunch the following Tuesday. After hearing about the system's first year, John called in a national leader to help his church with a similar program. Nine months of hard work flew by. During this period, every available evening was spent in calling on prospects. But it was worth it. The church had started to grow.

During the next year John refined and improved the calling system. The congregation continued to grow as people responded to the outgoing concern shown by church members. John's reputation soon spread to other churches. It wasn't long before he received a call to serve a much larger parish in a neighboring state. There he worked hard. After another four years he had proved that the same principles would work there. After a ten year decline, the church was growing.

For John, evangelism is a simple matter. Success comes from calling on people, making a lot of contacts. If you make enough calls, your church will grow. If you don't call, you don't grow. John doesn't understand why every preacher can't see this simple truth. For awhile, he worked aggressively to influence denominational leaders and clergy friends. If they would just adopt the programs he had found successful. . . . But most of them were unreceptive to his ideas. Finally he gave up the fight. People just weren't interested in evangelism he thought.

Wayne Porchet was in college during the escalating days of Vietnam. To submit to the draft in this questionable conflict was for him a true moral struggle. In these same years, he and many college friends were caught up in the Kennedy legacy and the Johnson dreams. It was an era of expansionism for hopeful social programs all across the nation. A sociology major, Wayne participated in a number of research projects whose results pointed the way toward healing change in a sick society. He thought it was a great day to be alive. He believed that the lot of American poverty dwellers and racial groups could be improved.

Through some quirk of fate, the lottery sieved him past the war. Happy to be spared the decision of whether to flee to Canada or not, his mind jumped in a new direction. While a college senior, he decided to prepare for the Christian ministry. Surely this profession was a good vantage point from which he could help propel society toward a better day.

On completion of seminary, Wayne became associate minister in a large city church. Their current crisis was whether to pick up their property valuation and flee to the fringe of the city, where most of their members now lived. During that first year the decision was made to stay, at least for a few more years. Wayne's primary job was youth work. In his spare time he would work with the minority people who had drifted into the shadow of this great old church. Through his own choice, Wayne's work soon overloaded toward social service. He organized new programs and became well-known to all community agencies. An innovative leader, he was always finding new money and methods to reach out to people with active concern.

Then one morning the phone rang. The national office was putting its hand on his shoulder. They needed someone like Wayne to help staff their Church and Society Division. He was articulate and imaginative. Surely he could help other congregations to get moving in the same creative directions he had discovered. Of course he would go.

Wayne, John, and George had never met. Then one day they were thrown together in a small discussion group at a state meeting. Directed to buzz about the previous speaker's presentation on evangelism strategy, they were to report back at the larger plenary session. Each was given opportunity to speak as the group fumbled for a consensus. All were amazed at the distorted ideas about evangelism held by the others. The only thing they could agree on was a list of opposite ideas. Privately, each departed the meeting vowing never to discuss evangelism again with anyone. You just can't make people see the real truth; they are too bullheaded.

Actually, each man was right and each was wrong. But all three together were more right than anyone was alone. Each method is certainly an important subdivision of the gospel message. But total specialization in any one of them is an invisible heresy of the twentieth century. Jesus didn't split the disciples into three departments and assign a section of the word to each. He sent his disciples out to *do* the Word by healing the sick, cleansing lepers, raising the dead, and casting out demons. They were to *be* the Word by keeping in contact with his Spirit through a strong prayer life. They were to *say* the Word by verbally proclaiming God's ever-present kingdom and inviting people to enter it.

Historically, compartmentalization of the word has been a recurring heresy. Monasticism furnishes a good example of the *being thread* of the word carried to extreme. The Christian Crusades of the twelfth and thirteenth centuries put great stress on the *doing* thread, though in a form quite different than the 1960s. And the Protestant Reformation majored in *saying the Word.* Each was a logical response to a particular set of needs, probably much more logical than each appears in the florescence of hindsight.

Such division of emphasis can even be detected among New Testament writers. They too, wrote from the perspective of a particular historical setting and personality inclination. Paul, for example, carries the freight for saying the Word. ". . . And how are they to believe in him of whom they have never heard? And how are they to hear without a preacher?" (Romans 10:14) The Book of James waves the banner for doing the Word instead of just talking about it. "So faith by itself, if it has no works, is dead." (James 2:17) The Gospel of John expounds long on being the Word, the need to develop the spiritual life. "Abide in me, and I in you. As the branch cannot bear fruit by itself, unless it abides in the vine, neither can you, unless you abide in me." (John 15:4)

This does not mean that New Testament authors specialized in one aspect of gospel to the exclusion of all others. It simply shows that personal gifts and environmental needs molded their inclinations too. So they became the vocal spokesman for that particular approach.

But all these diverse strands ended up in the stack of writings revered by early church leaders. And none is listed as superior to the others. So the custom of conveniently quoting only from those scriptures which support our pet approach is more than deceitful; it is unbiblical.

Part II

Saying the Word

3

CONTACT CEMENT

The most visible quality shared by growing churches is the large number of contacts they make each week with people outside their church. Finding a big list of people to contact takes a wide variety of forms. Some churches start with a community-wide telephone census. Some begin with block calling—door to door in a neighborhood. Others use the more traditional methods of Welcome Wagon list, utility companies, etc. Some (after growth begins) only have time to call on all the new families who register on pew forms each Sunday morning.

Most of the churches have a specific calling night each week. One has a group of ladies who call on all newcomers to the city on the fourth Tuesday of each month. In one case, the evangelism chairperson telephones people to assign calls that need to be made on other than specific calling nights. A church in Houston solicits representatives from each major subdivision in the community. That family calls on Sunday morning visitors who come from their subdivision. If the caller then feels that the pastor should visit, he is notified.

Calling used in all churches is brief in duration—twenty to thirty minutes—and carries the message of: "We are calling on behalf of the church, and also as your neighbor. We want to get to know you. We want you to know that we enjoyed having you visit the church."

Callers are recruited through a variety of methods. Some are signed up annually as a group of twelve or twenty-four people who commit a specific night each week to calling. Some churches use teams which rotate from month to month—Team A calling during October and Team B during November, etc.—thus avoiding troop exhaustion. Some churches give their callers elaborate and specific training; others simply ask them to get acquainted with people and let them know about positive aspects of the church.

All combinations of callers are used: Married couples; pairs of youth with youth, adults with youth, women with men; and individuals calling alone. One congregation even uses men and women who are not married to each other. Another uses a group of six to eight people who have recently joined the church. Each person then gives a one or two minute testimony about "why I joined this church." It is universally accepted that the newest members make the best callers. The bloom of their enthusiasm is still fresh. Their knowledge about the church's virtues has not yet been muddied with intricate information about problem areas.

A few churches do not make "decision calls," but wait for the people to say they wish to join. By far the majority do have some point in time (always after three or four other calls and only when the people have attended church several times) when they specifically ask prospects for a commitment to Christ and membership. In some congregations, a specific day of the month—like the first Sunday—is pushed as a day when many people will be joining the church. In other churches, every Sunday is advocated with equal energy. In most cases the "decision call" is preceeded by a letter from the pastor which says something like the following: "You've been attending our church. Evidently you like it. We're pleased about that. We'd love to have you as a member. Somebody will come by and talk with you about it."

Some pastors are convinced that a certain word formula is the most effective way to influence people toward decision. But a look at the various kinds of systems which are producing growth seems to indicate the contrary. As one pastor puts it, "It probably doesn't matter so much what you say. It may not even matter whether you say anything at all about the church. It only matters that you go. Then the people know that you care." Another says, "It is one thing to love God; another to love your neighbor. It takes love to go visiting strange people. But by being there you are saying, 'I care about you. I don't know how much I care yet. But I care about you.' And people respond to that caring."

Whatever form the calls take, repetition is another universal. Three to five calls, each by a different person or couple in the church, is the general rule. The church continues to assume that the people are interested (and keeps on calling) unless they get vibrations to the contrary. If so, the calls are discontinued and energy is directed elsewhere.

Along with personal calling, many other contact methods are used. One Oriental pastor of a small town Anglo congregation practices

25

what he calls "egg roll evangelism." Everyone who visits the church for the first time is invited to his home for an Oriental meal (one family at a time). During this getting acquainted experience he does not push the church—just gets to know them. The response has helped achieve their five year-131 percent growth rate.

That same congregation operates a unique Mother's Day Out Program which has proven to be an effective evangelism tool. Every Tuesday, forty families from across the town bring their children. Three different classes are held for age levels two, three, and four years old. With two teachers in each class, the program is more than baby sitting; it is Christian education. Many younger women who are new or prospective members help operate the event. Since it runs from nine to twelve o'clock, they don't need to worry about lunch, only a snack. This is even subsidized by picking up the children's birthdays each week so that mothers can be asked to bring a birthday cake. Very attractive to young couples with children, the program costs no money to operate. The $1.50 per day fee more than covers expenses.

All churches conclude that one of the easiest ways to find new members is to help them find you. Much free publicity is available in local papers by publishing news of congregational activities. One lady who had not been active in any church for several years said, "Every time I picked up the paper I read of something happening at your church. So I decided to come and find out if the programs were as exciting as they sounded." The couple joined within a month and have been actively involved ever since.

Signs at every edge of the parish or town are another asset. Metal models can be ordered from denominational headquarters, but they are second best. When dented and rusty with paint peeling, they are worse than none at all—saying more negative than positive about the church's welcome. Preferable to these are large attractive signs which capable lay members may be able to paint and letter themselves. One pastor says that bumper stickers are another possibility. Any why not? They are used for many less valid reasons. In a mobile society of two car families, they can provide a moving visibility at close to zero cost.

One congregation has a highly effective "Publicity Committee." It has the sole responsibility of telling the outside community that the church is alive, well, and ministering to people. The pastor in that church writes a column in the local newspaper and reports that a number of people visit the church after reading the column. He says that a lot of community newspapers are open to religious columns. In many cases all you have to do is ask.

A church marquee in West Texas said, "Plowing a field requires more than just turning it over in your mind." That truth goes deeper than agriculture. Whatever contact methods are used, *word* passing takes more than just thinking positive thoughts about the great commission. It requires going to real people with real front doors. Thinking about going or talking about going isn't enough. Yet this is the most prevalent reason for pigmy membership. The contacts simply are not made; thus, the influence cannot be felt.

A denominational task force defined evangelism as "sharing the Good News by being, doing, and saying." They went on to say that the Christian Church (Disciples of Christ) is probably "high on doing, medium on being, and low on proclaiming." A majority of Christian bodies would likely stack up under such a diagnosis. We have a great message—the greatest—but our verbal communication with potential receivers is infrequent.

A youth trudged into the college parking lot at the end of a snowy winter day. Getting into his "beetle," he noted a professor in trouble. Having left his lights on in the early morning sleet, his car wouldn't start. The battery was dead. Since the young man carried jumper cables in his trunk, it was easy to start the other car. All he had to do was attach the cables between the two batteries. But having the cables was not enough. Nothing happened until he touched the final clamp to the battery post. Nor is a good church, a shiny new building, a powerful preacher, and a lot of high voltage programs ever enough. Nothing happens unless you make contact with those outside the building.

Part of our contact failure accrues from a lack of perception about the starting point of all personality change. Remember the story of the man who hit his mule over the head with a two-by-four? When someone asked why he did that he replied, "First, I have to get his attention." That line speaks truth about human as well as mule nature. All behavior change begins with getting the mind's attention. Until people give their attention to a matter, their behavior will not begin to change regarding that matter.

God is constantly trying to get his children's attention. The primary way he succeeds is through the personality of his other children. Think back through your own life. What is your first memory of being influenced toward God? Was it not through some individual person that God touched your life? God can certainly work through nature, great architecture, outstanding literature, fine music, and personal experiences. But his most powerful tool is persons. The New Testament does not list any illustrations of people coming to the Christian faith except through the personality of another person.

Paul Tillich said, "Faith is a total and centered act of the personal self, the act of unconditional, infinite and ultimate concern."[1] But before that can occur, the mind must be directed toward these ultimate questions. And that seldom happens except through the influence of another human being.

Many people are waiting for someone to train them in some verbal karate chop. Then they will finally "know what to say to people." And some evangelism pros claim to possess such a weapon. But research in several growing churches indicates that such formulas are a superficial coating on something more basic. It is the personal contact that does most of the influencing, not the content of the contact.

27

People like Lewis Mumford and Marshall McLuhen have repeatedly said, "The medium is the message." The package in which the communication comes, like television, has more impact than what is actually said. In word passing, the medium is also the message. The content of what is voiced is often less important than the vehicle by which the content is transmitted.

John begins his Gospel by saying that the Word became *flesh*. (John 1:14) Notice that he doesn't say the Word was made *language*. That is what we try to accomplish with preaching, teaching, or writing. But God had already tried that with the prophets. It hadn't worked all that well. The Pharisees kept fouling it up with legalisms. So he sent a medium—his Son—who conveyed the message more clearly. The Word will never be incarnated in us as it was in Christ. But our contact with other people is still God's primary method of touching them with his love.

The word "witnessing" has been so overused that its meaning has blurred. What is a witness? Not necessarily one who knows *all* the facts in a particular court case. Sometimes he simply helps the jury to have faith in things which have already been said. He helps close the credibility gap on the unbelievable. Jesus was the faithful witness for God. He closed the credibility gap on what the prophets had already spoken. It is our task to do that for others.

Eating lunch in Cloudcroft, New Mexico, a man received his ticket from the waitress. Dawdling over his coffee, he turned it over absent-mindedly and read it thoroughly. At the bottom it said, "It has been a pleasure." Such words are printed on the back of most food service bills. But we generally don't see them, do we? Why not? Because they are too impersonal. Yet Christians use the same tactics and expect them to communicate. Church newsletters inviting people to worship are mailed out. A piece of stationery is sent, inviting people to attend a warm friendly church. But without the personal contact of people who care enough to send the very best—themselves—little influence is exerted.

A Church of Christ bulletin in Coldwater, Michigan, carried the story of a fellow who met a beautiful girl. He wanted to do some heavy courting so he bought 365 postcards, one for each day of the year. For twelve long months he sent her a love note each day. At the end of the year she got married, but not to him. She married the postman.

A record of the early Church says, ". . . And the Lord added to their number day by day those who were being saved." (Acts 2:47) God did the adding, not the preacher or the Apostles. But this just means the ability to create additions was not in their hands. Without the Christian presence in the Jerusalem community, additions would have been slim.

Why do we think anything can substitute for the personal touch? Sometimes because we are lazy. Sometimes because we don't care that much about other people. But more often because we have not done clearheaded homework. Sometimes we believe people are tired of being invited to church. Yes, new residents are often under siege for the first week after newcomer list publication. But when the fishing draws no attendance nibbles, they are written off as time wasters. Most unchurched people haven't had anybody call in their home for years.

Sometimes we think that common people like us are incapable of making good calls. But most of us possess more education than one of Jesus' best evangelists, Simon Peter. Evangelism is not as much a matter of saying the right thing as of making contact. Through that contact, attention focuses on God for a few minutes. Any kind of call can accomplish that, even if we use no words at all.

Take a tip from the most powerful influencers in the world, television ad men. First they get your attention with a brief presence in your home. What they say may sound silly, stupid, even irrational. But they do engage the attention of your mind. And that becomes a platform for influence towards whatever soup they are pushing.

Many callers worry about being pushy. "We don't want to offend people." We should be concerned about that. William Barclay says we probably don't have the right to confront a total stranger with "Are you saved?" He suggests that such a question may be as impertinent as asking for their bank balance. "A relationship has to be arrived at in which it is possible to talk of these things," he concludes. "But the great and grave danger is to lose the chance of talking about them at all."[2]

Christians have a powerful advantage that ad writers don't. They have the spirit of concern. Just as Jesus' love added power to the influence of his words, likewise does ours. Our chief equipment is not the fluent use of English but our spirit of concern for people. It is easy to blot out of your mind the man who came by to sell you a vacuum sweeper. Much harder to forget a person who goes out of his way to promote your interest in God.

A survey in Houston, Texas, asked why people joined one church in the community instead of another. Three percent said it was because of the beauty of the building; fourteen percent because it was the denomination of their prior affiliation; eighteen percent because of its convenient location near their home. But fifty-six percent came into that church because of the personal invitation of a member.[3]

That should not be news. Jesus didn't build a building. He didn't even ask people to flock together in the capital city to hear him preach. Nor did he buy a mimeograph and launch mass mailings. He wandered about the countryside making personal contact with all kinds of people: a harlot in the street; a short IRS agent in a tree; a fisherman by his boat; a woman drawing well water. "For the Son of man came to seek and to save the lost." (Luke 19:10) He didn't wait for them to find his address in the yellow pages. He did the walking himself.

Do we need buildings than? The church succeeded very well without them for the first 160 years. Should we burn the buildings instead of the mortgages and get back to their way of doing things? That would be as logical as disconnecting our air conditioners because they didn't have any. But there is constant danger that the center of the program become the whole program instead of the center for the program. It is never sufficient to stand up inside the building each week and ask, "Does anyone want to respond to Christ?" Jesus didn't say, "Meet me down at the corner, two doors down from the temple. I'll take you through an intensive course in religion." His question was never, "How can we relate these people to our movement?" His stance was, "How can I relate myself to these people?"

". . . pray therefore the Lord of the harvest to send out laborers into his harvest," Jesus said. (Luke 10:2) Note that he didn't ask for *smarter* workers but for *more* workers. He didn't demand seminary degrees, a B.S. in Social Science, or even church membership courses. He asked people for commitment to his cause, then sent them out to contact others. Our trend has flowed in the opposite direction. We have sought fewer contact persons, but better educated. Should we do the total opposite and assume that ignorance is a good evangelist qualification? No, but we do need to put more troops in the field and stop trying to hire well-trained generals to do it all.

Presence, verbalization, and concern are powerful influencers. But a fourth equally vital contact ingredient is often neglected—repetition. Driving west toward Tuscon, Arizona, on Highway 10 the tourist will see numerous large signs. The coming attraction is billed "The Thing," with several question marks intended to heighten the intrigue. Every few miles another sign appears—same words. This goes on for almost two hundred miles. Never are you told what "The Thing" actually is. But by the time you finally arrive at the driveway, it is difficult to resist turning in.

Any product that repeats its appeal in different ways at different times tends to bring a response. Why don't toothpaste firms buy thirty minutes of TV time once a month and give all their spot commercials in one lump? They understand the principle of repetition. We shouldn't commercialize Christ. There has already been too much of that. But we need to get smart about the psychology of human awareness. Thinking that "one call should be enough" is an illogical perception about how persons are influenced.

Acts indicates that Paul's primary evangelism technique was preaching. ". . . and how are they to hear without a preacher?" he inquires rhetorically of the Romans. (Romans 10:14) "So faith comes from what is heard, and what is heard comes by the preaching of Christ." (Romans 10:17) But we often overlook the convenient natural groupings into which Paul could project his message—the synagogue. ". . . they came to Thessalonica, where there was a synagogue of the Jews. And Paul went in, as was his custom, and for three weeks he argued with them from the scriptures. . . ." (Acts 17:1-2)

Paul had a perfect captive audience every Saturday. If he kept on traveling, he could find a new audience of nearly one hundred percent nonbelievers every week. Because he was a Jew and they were Jews—because he was a stranger and they were the hosts—they would hear him respectfully (at least for awhile). In a place where Paul didn't have a natural grouping—the Areopagus in Athens—things did not go nearly as well. (Acts 17:32)

That natural clustering of the "unChristed" does not occur in the present age. Sunday morning church is in no way similar to Paul's synagogue setup. Almost everyone here has heard the message one hundred times over. They may not be living it yet, but they have heard it. So if preaching is to get a hearing in our society, there must be some means of gathering a sympathetic crowd together. This situation pushes us into one-to-one evangelism methods for recruiting fresh listeners.

Some say that evangelism ought to be done during worship services only. This is convenient, but unbiblical. Personal contact techniques are less prominent in New Testament records because they were not needed as much. But when Paul was cut off from preaching, he did work with people one at a time. The jailers in various institutions are good examples. For illustrations other than Paul, see Phillip's conversation with a total stranger beside the interstate to Ethiopia. (Acts 8:30-31). Also note Phillip bringing Peter and Nathanael to be signed up as Apostles. (John 1:41, 45)

We are tempted to criticize the power failure in contemporary preaching. Yes, it may come partially from lack of inspiration, ability, and preparation. But it may have more to do with the kind of preachees against whom the *word* is thrown. We might better spend our time in trying to collect the kind of receptive audiences that Peter and Paul enjoyed at the height of their successes.

Few Christians will become preachers. (What a dull world it would become if they all did.) But all can help God bring people within earshot of the preacher's message. And is not this ministry as great as word proclamation? Unless receiving sets are brought close to the messengers, the message will go unheard. So what difference will it make how effectively they preach it? Words falling on absent ears are as futile as those landing on deaf ones.

After finding the value of personal contact, most pastors must pull some motivational tricks on themselves in order to maintain it. Sometimes the simplest ones are the most productive. One is to keep a continual chart of the number of calls made each week by pastor and people. Another minister found that he could increase church growth by keeping his prospect file on the front of his desk. When stored in the secretary's office where he seldom saw it, he made few calls. Keeping it on his desk kept the matter on his mind. So his mind more frequently got his body out on the sidewalk.

4
GOOD NEWS BY MODERN PERSONS

We began with the usual dentist-patient chitchat. But then he propped my mouth open with clamps and began to talk while I could not respond. I had to signal with my eyes or my hands, or just grunt. He told me about his theology and the church to which he belonged, saying that he felt most churches were completely missing the boat. After giving me a shot to deaden the pain, he said, "I'll be back in twenty minutes. I have to let this take effect."

Then he put earphones on me. They were attached to a little tape player that was timed just right. And he set it at a distance where I couldn't get up out of the chair to turn it off or unplug the earphones. The tape was various kinds of religious material which he apparently thought I needed.

This happened every time I went in for dental work. And it seemed as if the time I waited for the shot to take effect was so much longer than I ever had with other dentists. I told him that I was an active member of another church, but that didn't slow him down. Finally I told him in a joking way that I felt that I was being taken advantage of—not being given equal time—but it never made any difference. Finally I decided, "I've had enough of this." He was a good dentist, but I decided that I just wasn't going to pay for this kind of evangelism. So I started going to a dentist who wanted to fix my teeth instead of my religion.

This story from a Kansas church member is probably not what Paul meant when he wrote Timothy, ". . . preach the word, be urgent in season and out of season, convince, rebuke, and exhort, be unfailing in patience and teaching." (II Timothy 4:2) There is a big difference between objective witnessing and objectionable witnessing. The dentist couldn't see the double yellow line between the two.

A young mother spent eternal days and nights with a son recovering from brain tumor surgery. Days blurred into nights—nights blurred into forevers. Throughout the endless ordeal one particular nurse was different from all the others. The things she said encouraged the young mother to hold onto her shredded faith. She brought with her into the room a feeling that perhaps all would yet be well—God still cared about his children.

This frightened mother said that nurse influenced her toward God in a way that no minister ever had. How? She was not overly vocal about her faith. She didn't use a lot of religious words to communicate it. But her personality testified to spiritual connections at the core of her being. As Martin Luther put it, she was a "little Christ" for this young mother. Her personality presence was a communication tool through which God said his word.

The nurse probably lived closer to Paul's admonition to Timothy than did the dentist. And the way she did it clues us to the best manner for *word* passing anytime—a spirit of love and concern, acceptance and caring. Paul Tournier speaks about the "medicine of the person" as that attitude of doctor to patient which goes beyond the doctor's technical competence to communicate his personal concern.[1] People who intend to give the *word* to other people need a "medicine of the person" also. And therein lies the difference between objective telling and objectionable telling. One carries an air of "I have the truth and I insist on poking it down you." The other communicates a genuine concern.

On a flight to Dallas one night, a young man noticed that you can't see the propeller while the engine is running. It draws you forward into the night, but you can't see it. Then the plane began to drop out of the darkness toward the runways on the great Dallas-Fort Worth Airport, and the pilot turned on the landing lights. The prop could now be seen quite clearly. What had previously been invisible became a beautiful silver ark in the night. "So it is with God," he thought. "Mostly we can't see him at all, but sometimes someone turns the lights on for us. Some person or personality, and through them we can see that God is very real." And this all begins, not in the exact words people use with us, but the attitude they take toward us.

Jesus, the Word, was manifested to the Apostles as a man. In the present age we think of him as manifested in three primary ways: (1) the Holy Spirit, (2) the words of the New Testament, and (3) the personality of other people. But we often feel that when God uses personality, it is only that of the preacher in the pulpit. Wrong! Preaching is certainly an important word power line, but casual conversations can often do just as much.

A man purchased a pocket Bible from the rack in a church reception area. When he asked for the price, the secretary said, "That will be forty cents."

"Forty cents," he said in astonishment. "That is the best bargain I've had in years. Just think, to get the word of God for only forty cents."

But God has provided an even cheaper way to get his word across—human personality and conversation. What the American Bible Society can print for forty cents, God does free. His newest and best translation is the *word* he writes on human personality.

A young woman in the clutches of depression was spending an evening at the public library. Flipping idly through the pages of a book about Eskimos, she scanned several paragraphs. Then a sentence unexpectedly jumped off the page and cleared the cobwebs from her brain. "People are happy who are doing what they are cut out to do. Their circumstances have little to do with their state of happiness." Those words became the *word* for her. They gave her insight about herself that she hadn't been able to see. For her, they were as much a revelation from God as Moses' burning bush. From that small beginning, she took action to set her life in new directions.

Those who handle words in pulpits know that this can happen to people in pews. There, the spoken word often becomes the life-transforming word. But pew residents usually don't realize that their words can do the same thing for others. And not just at the times when they use holy language. We don't constantly have to thread religious jargon through our conversational needles in order for God to make *word* out of words. In fact, he can often work through nonreligious language better than pious platitudes. What seems like casual utterance can become in that moment the word for a human predicament. When we finally understand that, we understand ourselves to be what God has called us to be—potential transmitters of new life to those around us. Not every contact will produce this impact. But knowing it can happen helps keep us alert to the power of our life, our presence, our attitude, our personality.

In a Massachusetts hospital, a woman with liver failure was recently treated by a rare medical method. Her total blood supply was cross-

34

circulated through the body of a man who lay dying from a fatal brain injury. Through this process his liver was able to cleanse her blood. She regained consciousness, became alert and communicative, and eventually recovered. God did that for us in Christ. Because of his life, God's Word got through to us. And it is through our life that God gets through to most other lives.

What kind of words should we use to become more effective servants of the word? Is there some magic formula that ought to be passed around? Paul put it this way, "Be wise in the way you act toward those who are not believers, making good use of every opportunity you have. Your speech should always be pleasant and interesting, and you should know how to give the right answer to every person." (Colossians 4:5-6 TEV) While we can't be certain we will always give the right answers, we can fulfill the first part of the formula—being pleasant (which means accepting and non-judgmental). Having fulfilled that, the second part will take care of itself. Word transmission is never so much a matter of giving empirical truth as of giving emotional acceptance. Some materials, like copper, are good electrical conductors. Some are poor conductors, like wood. Some kind of people are good conductors of the Word; some are poor. And you can divide the two kinds by measuring their ability to communicate love, acceptance, and a non-critical conversational pattern. In other words, grace.

A certain minister has such a warm loving personality that people are instantly attracted to him. He is inclined to spotlight their virtues and overlook their flaws. So they bring personal problems to him that they would never think of broaching to anyone else. Through this power of love and acceptance, he has drawn thousands of people to God and gospel. While he, as a pastor, has a unique opportunity to do this, every Christian has that potential. Warm personalities that communicate grace-acceptance-forgiveness constitute God's latest translation. They are *Good News by Modern Persons* for redeeming his children from their lesser selves.

The communication of grace in conversation does not arise from a memorization of psychological counseling techniques. It comes from the spiritual experience of grace at the center of personality. A preacher said during the informal moments of a worship service, "This ritual of friendship and fellowship is made possible by our Lord Jesus Christ." Accurate at more than one location. Authentic, loving, accepting warmth is a by-product of the Spirit of Christ clothed in human personhood. Without that inner experience, all the conversational techniques in psychology won't make people grace transmitters. This does not mean that training in how to relate to people should not be sought and learned. But if this becomes our only appeal, we become ventriloquist dummies rather than Christian witnesses. Friendliness practiced only as a mechanical method makes the right motions but succeeds at superficiality.

Whatever method we use, it will involve contact with people and the use of words. Without some kind of words, the *Word* seldom reproduces. Paul, in describing his encounter with Jesus on the Damascus Road, reports that Jesus told him, "I am Jesus, whom you persecute. But get up and stand on your feet. I have appeared to you to appoint you as my servant; you are to *tell* others what you have seen of me today, and what I will show you in the future." (Acts 26:15-16 TEV) Paul is told to go and *tell*. No mention is made of using the commonly proposed "let your light so shine" method. What if Paul had stayed silently in Jerusalem for thirty years developing his spiritual life and doing good deeds for people? This does not negate those virtues. But it does illustrate their inability to produce new Christians in most situations. Spiritual living and practical good works should be done. But they will not evangelize Averagetown, U.S.A., anymore than they would have worked in Rome or Corinth.

There is such a thing as nonverbal communication. "Body language" sometimes tells chapters that words leave out. And the church has body language too, which often speaks loudly. But without what comes from the mouth, body language leaves us trying to figure out what the person really meant. The same results when we try to communicate the word without talking to people. We don't need a tape recorded message, but we will need words. As Tillich has observed, ". . . the act of faith, like every act in man's spiritual life, is dependent on language and therefore on community. . . . Without language there is no act of faith, no religious experience!"[2]

The word gospel means "good news." Good news can usually be seen and photographed, and can often be felt with your fingers. But more than anything else, it is vocal—something you tell. Paul went into Asia Minor telling something new, not just living something new. He didn't go to do good deeds, but to say good news. Like Jesus, Paul lived a spiritual life that authenticated his words. He did loving acts like taking an offering for the starving in Judea. (Acts 11:29-30) But he never tried to substitute the deeds for the words. The predominant characteristic of his ministry was his insistence on speaking about Christ. That's what kept him in jail all the time, and ultimately cost him his life. The last line of biographical detail about him describes his residence in a rented house in Rome for two years. Awaiting trial for his life, he welcomed all who came there and taught them about Jesus Christ, "speaking with all boldness and freedom." (Acts 28:31 TEV)

Little is accomplished in this world without the use of words. Imagine a used car salesman without words. Imagine a store clerk without words. Imagine a radio announcer speechless. The Bible is called the word of God. The gospel is not called the good example or the good method or the good way; but the *good news.* God does not draw many people to himself through the example of a sunset, the promise of a rainbow, or the silent testimony of a microscope. Some, yes, but not many. Mostly he does it through the word of the prophet, the word of Christ, the word of the Apostles. And if we intend to influence anyone toward God, we are not likely to do it without words. We will at least have to learn to say something like, "We sure would like to have you come to church."

In the assembly room of the United Nations Building in New York City, all the seats are equipped with earphones. If the Japanese delegate is speaking, you probably wouldn't understand him. But if you put on the earphones and set the dial for English, you will hear his words in your own language. Someone in the control room is translating the Japanese into English. This is what the Christian does for God, He is a word translator. You may have trouble understanding Paul's intricate theology in Romans. The difficult analogies and symbolisms of John in Revelation appear complex. But God has better methods than this for communicating himself to the world. He chooses bookkeepers, corporation executives, schoolteachers, and real estate agents to thrust himself into every segment of society. These people can get it said in ways that people can understand.

A boy growing up on a dairy farm in Illinois spent mornings and evenings in the barn. One thing that lightened those hours of work was an old dusty radio. At the station breaks the announcer would always say, "This is W.L.S. Chicago, your clear-channel station." Being a clear-channel station meant their transmitting power was so great that you could always hear them loud and clear. But one day the old radio went on the blink. All it could utter was static. The boy's father observed, "I guess it must have a short-circuit."

Most people in our town will not meet God unless he is somehow communicated through us and our words. What if we are speechless about God in our daily conversation? What if we are afraid? What if we are embarrassed? What if we don't have the time? How then will God get his word across? "So we are embassadors for Christ, God making his appeal through us. . . ." (II Corinthians 5:20) What if his ambassadors do not go? And what if they cannot talk?

5
SAINTS UNDER CONSTRUCTION

One summer morning a junior high boy was walking to Sunday church school. He was alone because his parents never went anyplace with him. In fact, they seldom went anywhere together, except perhaps to a bar. About a half block from the church, he was engaged in conversation by an adult member from the church of his destination. The man asked why he was dressed in blue jeans. Getting insufficient answer, he lectured the lad on the necessity of coming to church in proper attire. "After all, God expects us to look our best for him," was his clinching logic.

When they got to the front lawn of the church, the boy excused himself. Saying he had forgotten his Bible, he doubled back toward home. He never went back to that church. In fact, he didn't go back to any church for more than fifteen years. Blue jeans were the only kind of trousers he owned. When he finally told someone this story, it was a minister doing parole counseling for state prison releasees.

In another congregation, two little boys were clowning around in the sanctuary between Sunday school and church time. The well-meaning elder who caught them at it shouted, "What the hell are you boys doing up there?" The tongue-lashing that followed sounded strangely inappropriate.

A worried mother came out of the hospital's intensive care ward. Her daughter had been there for six days following an automobile accident. Having just regained consciousness, she was complaining that her back ached. The first person the mother encountered in the waiting room was a good friend who inquired how the girl was doing. Pleased that her daughter was now conscious, the mother recounted the story of rubbing her back in order to help relieve the pain.

"Oh, you didn't rub her back, did you?" interrupted the friend in a scolding tone. "You're not supposed to massage or anything else unless you ask the nurse. You may have injured her. Did you ask the nurse?"

What this clumsy friend said may have been accurate. But on a list of the ten crudest things available to say, this would have ranked near the top. Yet she appeared not to recognize her remarks for what they were.

In the spiritual hospitals we call churches, how often similar careless statements are thrown by the saints at the not-yet saints. Some school teachers have the inate ability to make students hate chemistry or English for all eternity. And some graceless personalities throw so much mud on the *word* that strangers are inspired to run in the other direction. This doesn't mean Christians should vote in favor of moral anarchy. We should not encourage people to live by principles inconsistent with God's obvious expectations. But with a half ounce of tact, it is possible to affirm people without affirming their poor behavior.

Jesus did that. The woman taken in adultery, the multi-married lady, and Zacchaeus—all are random samples of his approach to people: concern in spite of rejection of their bad behavior. By this method he was able to lift up the same people the Pharisees had only alienated.

A student minister had more enthusiasm than perception of small town attitudes. So he started a Saturday evening ministry at the local bar. Drinking coffee while others followed other inclinations, he discovered what bartenders already know. People talked with him about problems there in a corner booth who would never have thought of knocking on his study door. This method proved too risky for his self-preservation in that parish, but he had the right idea. He was doing a Jesus thing: affirming the not-yet saints.

A young woman in one super-growing congregation said, "I think a large growing church is a lot more friendly than a small congregation that isn't. In a growing church, many people are new. So they are sensitive to the needs of new people. They remember how it feels to be new, and they work a lot harder at making people feel welcome." The reverse seems true in many ungrowing churches. Members are often insensitive to the needs of new or visiting families.

In a small town church latecomers were straggling in to prepare for an evening fellowship dinner. Pies were being "rowed" up, salads uncovered; fried chicken aroma filled the basement area. Here and there groups of people were collected in idle conversation. Over to one side several men exchanged ideas about corn prices and weather. Across the room, clusters of women were comparing recipes and complaining about grocery prices.

The pastor had been busy that week. In several calls on prospective members, he had encouraged them to attend the dinner. "It is a good opportunity for you to get acquainted," he told them.

One young couple, much to his surprise, took him seriously. But when he arrived late, after an emergency hospital call, he saw instantly that none of the men had made the least effort to talk with their stranger guest. A shy person, he was leaning against a wall, staring into space. His wife was trying to look included by eavesdropping on a nearby cluster of women. Quickly sizing up the situation, the pastor hurried over to engage the man in conversation. But the couple never came back to another fellowship dinner, or to a church service.

Along with this unintended social non-acceptance, many groups throw up more obvious roadblocks. "If we can just get people to change their ideas about morality. If we can just get them to drop their drinking habits, their smoking habits, their something habits; they might make good church members. But I can't feel good about having someone like that in our church."

There is certainly value in high moral standards for church members. But it is precisely the virtue in such ideals that blinds us to their half-truth. Trying to get people to "have the mind of Christ" on moral matters is admirable. (I Corinthians 2:16) But we must always be wary that we are not really trying to get them to "have our mind" on the matter instead of his. Many who think they are witnessing to God's word are really trying to speak God's words for him. That subtle sort of idol worship (idolatry of moral systems) tries to take over God's job of being God. "Accept among you the man who is weak in the faith, but do not argue with him about his personal opinions," (Romans 14:1 TEV) is still excellent advise. Pride in our own righteousness has no place in *word* communication.

Paul sent the Galatian church a letter warning against trust in such good qualities as circumcision. "It does not matter at all whether or not one is circumcised," Paul says. "What does matter is being a new creature." (Galatians 6:15 TEV) The Galatian approach to faith was insidious because it looked so righteous. How could it be bad to force new Christians to comply with an Old Testament law? But that is what makes most legalisms so dangerous. They look like a good thing.

So their advocates overlook the best thing—love—in their preoccupation with that good thing.

It is easy to see how the Galatians got hung up on the circumcision issue. After all, they were stressing one of the great trademarks of their ancient faith. This rite had been meaningful for at least twelve hundred years. Such mistakes have been made in every century, most of them by well intentioned people. The Spanish Inquisition, for instance, pushed purity over the edge of its sanity. "You make a good church by killing all the people who don't think like you do." Yet their total non-love appeared as a virtue to themselves. How easy to see that elder brother extreme in them; how difficult in ourselves.

When Paul uses the word "saints" in his salutation to the Corinthians, he doesn't mean "perfect ones" as some imagine. He means people who are "set apart." This is a good thing. Otherwise, few would have qualified to read the letter. His group of saints at Corinth were certainly not bumping their halos on door frames. If Paul had handled the saints at Corinth according to strict legalism, he would have written them out of the church instead of writing them a letter.

At a little town in Iowa, the visiting preacher was amazed by an incongruous sign in front of the asphalt parking spaces. "No Parking" it said in stark black letters. There must have been some good explanation for the sign. Perhaps it was erected to prevent accidents on that busy street. But he wondered if the members realized how inappropriate it looked. Probably not. Many congregations have invisible theological or emotional "no parking" signs which turn people away from the love of Christ.

"Let us then pursue what makes for peace and for mutual upbuilding," Paul says to the Romans. (Romans 14:19) And many who set up arbitrary behavior standards are trying to do just that—upbuild someone. But how easy it is to think our words are making someone better when they are only making him bitter. A few lines later, Paul adds, "Accept one another, then, for the glory of God, as Christ has accepted you." (Romans 15:7 *Good News for Modern Man*) And that involves restraint in telling them how dumb or irreligious they are. They are probably already aware of those imperfections. The good news of the gospel is that God loves them anyway. And one of the quickest ways they can become aware of that good news is by learning that one of God's children can love them anyway.

Preaching, teaching, and the Holy Spirit are more than sufficient to let people know they are far away from God. He does not need help from us in getting his message of judgment across. What he does need is our personality to serve as vehicle for his redeeming love. When we act in that service, we are acting like Christ. ". . . for I did not come to judge the world but to save the world." (John 12:47) Grace was his approach to people, not judgment. And if we use his perspective, we are likely to get his result—a positive response. The church was intended to be a redemptive community, not a religious supreme court. If we insist on acting like the Pharisees, we will reap their harvest—a chance to say some brilliant and cutting things to people, but rarely the opportunity to see human lives changed to their highest potential.

Samuel Shoemaker observed that "Some Christians are close to God, but remote from people; some are close to people, but remote from God; some are close to neither; and *some are close to both.* Those who are near to God and to their fellows are the real fishers of men."[1] How does one get close to his fellows? Certainly not by harangues; certainly not by criticizing them.

Conversationally, the words "I understand" come closest to the redeeming grace that was Jesus' approach. Carl Rogers has repeatedly pointed out the healing power in these two words. He and others have developed a whole school of psychotherapy designed to teach counselors how to say that and then shut up. God can similarly use ordinary Christians to draw persons to their higher selves in himself. Many adults experienced no love and acceptance as a child. So they go through the rest of their life looking for it. Christ is the answer to that basic need. And the main way his love begins to come through is in the form of an accepting human being.

"How can I witness to Christ without acting as if I am judging people?" Christians ask. With love! Simply express in your own words the value of your own personal experiences with Christ and his Church. Do this in love and acceptance, without trying to change the other person. Get them into the church. Get them close to Christ. He will do the changing; you won't have to.

A layman in one growing church says, "Our church is an accepting church. We accept people for the way people are, and we leave the judgment up to God. A couple, for instance, comes to our church who are living together out of wedlock. We accept them. I think anybody in this community who chooses to visit or join our church would be accepted by all the membership. If an individual comes in who was drunk the night before, and his eyes are bleary, I'm going to accept him. I think that's what God wants us to do, regardless of what he has done in the past, or what he is doing right now."

A minister in another church said, "My concept of authentic humanness is to help people to become 'perfect as your Father in heaven is perfect.' And God is so perfect that he can allow imperfection. That's real perfection."

A minister was amazed to recognize a young man on TV doing an automobile commercial. It was the same boy with whom he had done parole counseling several years before. A successful burglar, he had been caught only two times out of forty-five robberies. A few days later the minister was traveling through the town where the man was now living, so he looked him up. Well dressed, happily married, a successful businessman, how different he was from the boy of years before. "How did it all happen?" the minister asked.

"I guess maybe it was my boss. He got me started going to church and. . . ."

A middle-aged man in Kentucky had been a dedicated alcoholic for years. In partnership with his uncle, the two were constantly quarreling. The business had deteriorated from his overattention to glass bottles. A minister worked with the man for three years, trying to encourage him toward Christ. But he failed. When the pastor moved away, he was sure that this man would never change. But several years later a friend's letter informed him that the man was now an elder in the church. He had stopped drinking, stopped chasing women, and was now taking responsibility for his business.

You would have thought Paul was a finished product too. A mature man, his profession was portable district attorney for the Pharisees. But it was after this that he became a radically different person. And take a look at yourself. Are you the person you were ten years ago? Would you want people to judge you by the amount of maturity you had at that stage of your development? There are some aspects of personality that remain much the same throughout the years. But the good news about people is that they can change.

This doesn't mean all changes will be for the good. People are sometimes converted from good to bad as well as from worse to better. But they are always *capable* of being converted to something better. Because of this potential, acceptance of where people are right now is the only rational attitude. We don't yet know what a person—any person—may become. We do know that if we judge them and put them down, they are likely to become less than they are. For people respond to judgment by getting worse. But if we issue them (in spite of their obvious flaws) the kind of grace Christ gave us, they may rise up with wings as eagles. For humans tend to respond to love and acceptance by getting better.

A high school boy named Draper was not very good looking. Overgrown and overweight, he was awkward as a turtle. From his clothing to his P.E. class, he never seemed to fit anything. John Draper could easily have won the trophy for the senior most likely to fail at just about everything. But a classmate picked up the hometown paper the other day. John's picture was on the front page. He is now a nuclear scientist, one of the top men in our national defense program. Never accept any person for what they are right now. You don't know what they may become.

Part III

Doing the Word

6

LOVE IS AN INSIDE JOB

A young seminarian was in hospital chaplaincy training at a large city hospital. One of the first patients he met on his assigned floor was a middle-aged insurance salesman. This man was a real evangelist, but not for the church. Having been an alcoholic for years, eight months ago he had joined Alcoholics Anonymous. At every opportunity he would saturate the young theologian with the values of that organization—how important it was and how much it meant to him—how much the members had done to help him out of his trouble.

Late one afternoon a page interrupted the chaplain trainee's coffee break in the hospital cafeteria. Picking up a nearby phone, he was requested to go to his floor. The insurance agent patient urgently wanted to see him. He couldn't imagine what it might be about. They had just had a long talk that morning when he made rounds.

Arriving at the room, he found the man anxiously waiting to show him some flowers that had just been delivered. He asked the chaplain to read the card. It was from his AA group. "Now that's what I mean," the man said excitedly. "That's what makes the difference. Those fellows really care something about me."

During the course of the conversation that followed, the chaplain asked him why it was that people didn't feel that way about their church.

"People do not have the fellowship in the church that they have in AA" he replied. "They just don't care about each other that much."

He was accurate about many congregations. Bartenders extend more genuine concern for people than is expressed in some churches. Members often find more Christian love in their offices, clubs, and lodges than inside the building dedicated to the Lord of love.

The energy crisis in Christian charity does not begin with followers of Jesus unwilling to love their neighbors in the ghetto, on the Jericho Road of poverty-stricken Appalachia, or in starving Nigeria. The love deficiency starts with failure to love each other inside the church. Jesus told his disciples to ". . . love one another; even as I have loved you. . . ." (John 13:34) Without that, encouragement to "do it to one of the least of these my brethren . . . , in prison . . . , starving . . . , or naked . . . ." (Matthew 25:40-43) will pass through heads like a blank computer card. Only when people start loving each other inside can they start loving others outside.

Some people think the reverse is true; that if we mobilize the saints to help the less fortunate, then they will start loving each other as a secondary result of doing those good things together. That can happen, and has happened. But there appear to be more pastors holding that theory in their heads than real life places where the theory is working. The concrete evidence points toward the likelihood that strong social involvement by a congregation is usually preceded by a strong relationship of affection within the church. Authentic fellowship of the saints appears to be the best early preparation for ministry to the not-yet saints.

We know this is true in personality. Psychologists assure us that persons incapable of loving and respecting themselves will have difficulty extending unselfish love toward others. And those who try to reach into community and world without building a loving congregation face eternal frustration. It is in learning to love one another that we learn how to love strangers. Pastors who strive for end results without going through prior causes are like a man who tries to grow apples without a tree. He will get very frustrated. In fact, he may one day decide to drop out of the apple business altogether.

Elton Trueblood wisely observed that we cannot have fruits without roots.[1] One of the fruits is the shaping of political and community structures in Christian directions. The roots, of course, begin in our relationship to the loving Christ. But something must connect the roots and the fruits: the tree. That organism is the congregation, which by receiving grace from the roots, both sustains itself and produces fruit.

It is natural that we should become preoccupied with getting Christians out on the street to help people. There are such obvious human needs all around us. But doing social love to the exclusion of all else becomes "mule work." Mules have great stamina; are capable of pulling enormous loads. Unfortunately, mules are sterile. They do not reproduce themselves. If we depend on social action to create new Christians, we will discover a decreasing amount of good work being accomplished. And for the same reason.

"So then, as we have opportunity, let us do good to all men, and especially to those who are of the household of faith." (Galatians 6:10) Paul's injunction definitely supports loving actions directed to those outside the church. This blows out the circuits of those who say we should not meddle in society structures. There is no place where Christians have more business than in trying to bind up wounds inflicted by demonic forces in high places. But Paul says, ". . . especially to those of the household of faith." That equally destroys the theory of those who advocate doing *nothing but* improving societal systems. Our love should cut in both directions at once: (1) toward those inside the church who may not deserve it because they are polished hypocrites, and (2) to those outside the church who are often hardheaded and intentional non-saints.

Doing the Word in concrete ways is definitely part of the gospel. In Jesus' story of the sheep and the goats, the final reward goes to the doer, not to the talker. The verbalist ends up in hell, and there seems no way to interpret away the clear meaning of that. (Matthew 26:46) Along with instructions to preach, Jesus told the twelve to, "Heal the sick, raise the dead, cleanse lepers, cast out demons." (Matthew 10:8) He told the rich young ruler to ". . . go, sell what you have, and give to the poor, . . . and come, follow me." (Mark 10:21) "The religion of love as taught by Jesus is no philosophical theory of knowledge," says Kagawa. "If we would see God, we must first love."[2]

But we must keep on asking two great questions with equal drive and interest: (1) What unmet human needs exist right here in River City which our congregation might be able to fill? (2) What needs exist right here in our own members? Food, shelter, and clothing do not make up the entire need range of human beings. "Man shall not live by bread alone. . . ." (Matthew 4:4) We forget that because the bread needs are so obvious other needs are often invisible—sheltered within the personality. People in our churches also need things: emotional security, recognition and reassurance of worth, creative outlets, a sense of belonging, affection. Jesus cared deeply about people—all kinds of people—both his beloved disciples and strangers at wells. He worked with equal patience among hardheaded Peters and lost sheep of Israel.

Most pastors major in one or the other of these two equally important kinds of love. Usually because they find that particular brand more suited to their personal talents, or just plain more fun. One preacher said he would rather go to an AA meeting than to a prayer meeting because people were more honest there. Another worked actively to influence state legislators because that was much more exciting and prestigious than pastoral calling. Others would rather take a pie to a shut-in and call it a day. That is much less work than trying to change some of the structures by which our culture kicks its neighbors when they are down. To do either without the other is Christian neglect. To do either and intentionally neglect the other is Christian heresy. To do neither is not Christian at all.

The "good works hobbyhorse" is a tempting trip. Some go for ego purposes or simply to fulfill their own internal program outline. "On that day many will say to me, 'Lord, Lord, did we not prophesy in your name, and cast out demons in your name, and do many mighty works in your name?' " (Matthew 7:22) Bonhoeffer reminds us, "At this point Jesus reveals to his disciples the possibility of a demonic faith which produces wonderful works quite indistinguishable from the works of the true disciples, works of charity, miracles, perhaps even of personal sanctification, but which is nevertheless a denial of Jesus and of the life of discipleship."[3]

"Let your light so shine before men, that they may see your good works and give glory to your Father who is in heaven," Jesus tells his disciples. (Matthew 5:16) It isn't just good works that are advocated. It is good works for the purpose of drawing people to God. The great temptation is to let our light shine in such a way that people will think of *us* rather than of God. Giving in to that seduction can drive us to love people where it has the highest public visibility—outside the church.

Others get hung up in the internal versus external love argument for a more obscure reason. They aren't really inclined to love in either direction. Thus, talking about it becomes an escape from doing it. Love as a discussible feeling substitutes for love in coveralls.

A young man spoke to a counselor about the most painful hours of his life: the time he spent at the front window watching for his parents' car to turn in the driveway; crying because it didn't. Very wealthy, his father was hog-tied with business; his mother trapped in the social swirl. They employed a cook to fix meals, dust the furniture, and raise the kids. The only time he saw his parents was an occasional morning when his dad overslept and his mother got up early. On those days, he accidently met them at the breakfast table. This sometimes happened once a week or more. This boy's parents, if asked whether they loved him, would have said they did. But did they?

We can see the difference between feeling and action here. But it is much harder to see the difference in ourselves or inside the church. A teenager came home from choir practice early one evening. His father was incredulous. The boy had never come home early from anything.

Looking over his paper he asked, "What brings you back so soon?"

"We had to call off choir practice for this week," the youth replied. "The organist and the choir director got in a terrible argument about how to sing 'Love Divine,' so we quit for tonight."

The exact meaning of an idea is often lost in the translation between languages. This is especially true as the word love travels from the Greek Bible to the mind's English. "Do unto others as you would have others do unto you." (Matthew 7:12 paraphrase) Jesus doesn't tell us to *think* about other people as we would have them think about us. Nor does he tell us to *feel* about other people as we would want them to feel about us. He tells us to *do*. When Jesus used the word love, he was talking about an action you take toward someone, not a feeling you have for them.

"For God so loved the world that he gave his only Son. . . ." (John 3:16) He didn't just sit around heaven feeling badly about his wayward children. He sent his Son to care for them. "This is my commandment, that you love one another as I have loved you." (John 15:12) In the very next verse, Jesus mentions giving up his life for his friends. On the cross he lives out his definition of love; an action.

Love like his is always an active verb; never a passive noun that stands around like a statue doing nothing. If what we feel for other people is nothing but a warm fuzzy, we are not talking about Christian love. We may be talking about selfishness, ego, or pride which often masquerades as love. But we aren't talking about what Jesus did.

The February bulletin board for a day school kindergarten claimed colorfully, "Valentines Speak of Love." And that is significant—to speak of love verbally is important. But love is not really a feeling; it is an action.

All growing churches have found numerous concrete ways to keep this kind of action between members at a high and constant level. "It is our hope that people visiting will notice the difference," says one pastor. " 'How those Christians love each other' is the reputation we seek."

7
GATHERING TWO
OR THREE

Two cousins went crappie fishing on a lake down in Missouri. Crappie are small, but good eating if you get enough of them. Instead of bothering with a troublesome stringer, the children took a burlap sack to put the fish in. After an exceptionally good afternoon, they were walking proudly back to the house. One carried the fishing poles. The other shouldered the sack containing more than one hundred fish.

Sensing that his partner had stopped, the boy leading the way through the brush turned to see why. His friend was looking back in consternation at the route they had just traveled. Here and there in the grass was an unusual sparkle. Looking closer, they saw an uneven trail of fish all the way back to the lake. Putting down his sack, the boy poked his finger through a hole in the bottom.

"Fishers of men" (Mark 1:17) often have identical experiences. Many of their converts join the church with enthusiasm, attend for a few weeks or months, then gradually slack off and fall out. Membership rolls are packed with such people, who are rarely thought of more than once a year. We might not remember them then, but we have to count the inactive members for the denominational annual report.

Membership conservation must not be confused with evangelism, anymore than fishing should be confused with a fish fry. But church growth involves stopping up the holes in our sack as well as getting the fish into the sack to start with.

We cannot deal with this problem effectively until we begin to understand what people are looking for when they join a church. There is certainly more than one item on this list. New members are seeking such things as a place to give their children Christian education; a good preacher; teachings that will enrich their lives; opportunities for meaningful service to others; a nice building in a convenient location. Some of the minor reasons would be as miscellaneous as people themselves. Several men will remember joining a church because their girl friend (who became their wife) grew up in it.

But beyond these multiple reasons, is there any one thing that *everyone* is looking for in church membership? The answer can be couched in one word: *acceptance*. If we use the biblical word we would say "love," but Hollywood has tarnished that syllable into vagueness. Another good word is koinonia, but since most people don't read Greek, that doesn't communicate as well as we preachers think. People are looking for a church where they can find a warm relationship with other people. They are looking for people who care about each other and will give them an opportunity to become a part of the group. Everyone wants to be wanted. And churches who do a good job of meeting this universal human need retain a "high fish to skillet" ratio.

When people drop out of a church (or don't drop in), it is often due to a lack of such warmth and acceptance. To put it another way, lack of genuine Christian fellowship experiences. A seminary professor tells the story of camping with his children beside a lake in New Mexico. While he pitched the tent, the children began making new friends with children in another family camped nearby. For awhile all the children seemed to play well together—everyone was included. But then he noticed a boy smaller than the others being left out. In his left out feeling the little boy cried, "I am here. I am here. Can't anybody see that I'm here."

When new church members feel this way, they don't cry out. They just fade out, and you can rarely get them to verbalize exactly why. Usually it is because they never felt really accepted. But sometimes even they themselves do not realize this. Their subconscious finds other complaints to express, so they won't have to deal with the emotional pain involved. We must not deduct from this that the church members of long standing do not *want* to accept new members. Their non-acceptance is usually not from a lack of sincerity or concern. More often, it is a shortage of any effective acceptance *structures* within the church.

Some will charge that those who dropped out "simply weren't committed to start with." Sometimes true, but the reverse is more often the case. Converts whose relationship and acceptance needs are not met often wither away before they can begin to develop strong commitment in the faith. New converts don't begin with maturity; they begin with a decision to seek maturity. Their involvement in strong fellowship-acceptance groups then muscles and nurtures their decision into stronger commitment.

At Pentecost, the course of development was: (1) faith in Jesus Christ, (2) incorporation into church life, (3) a deepening of the original commitment through fellowship with the saints, and (4) involvement in various forms of mission and service according to the personal gifts (skills) of each member. Whether the Apostle Paul or minor convert, the individual found Christian growth through Bible study, prayer, communion, and common fellowship. (Acts 2) We do not find any New Testament records of strong Christians developing alone. Unlike some other world religions, Christianity has always been a group affair. "For where two or three are gathered in my name, there am I in the midst of them." (Matthew 18:20)

Here is another of those many points at which successful nurture and effective evangelism methodologies overlap. The same kinds of group programming which help new members find acceptance-fellowship also help to attract more new members. So developing good group life in the church is not just a method for keeping the fish; it is also a good means of catching them to start with.

There is no one system of group work, prayer circle, or Bible study used by all growing congregations. One large church has thirty-five adult Bible study groups meeting weekly. Another forms new share groups two or three times a year. Couples have the opportunity to meet once a week for six to eight weeks with subject matter drawn from a wide variety of topics. Another involves many members in some type of community service work. Even within the same church, a wide diversity of study, fellowship, and service opportunities seems to be the norm. As one pastor puts it, "We feel it is important to have a variety of things happening around the church every week. You must involve different people in different things, meeting them where they are."

Such diversity of group work probably tells us that the type of study material and meeting methods are not the key here. It is the opportunity to be together, share with each other, learn from each other, and draw mature strength from each other that meets a universal human need.

At no age level is programming quality and diversity more essential than with teenage youth. Someone wrote to the *Church Management* magazine's question and answer column asking, "If our church is to

51

grow and be healthy, what age group should we focus attention on?" The reply was, "Forty-six percent of the United States population is under age 25. That should give you a clue. . . ."[1]

Every growing church has effective youth programs which involve a large number of young people in a smorgasbord of ways: (1) strong music programs of various kinds for various age levels; (2) in-depth biblical, spiritual, psychological, help-type input; (3) strong Sunday morning church school programs; (4) frequent recreational opportunities; and (5) service opportunities.

The most effective programs are those which allow young people to plug in according to their needs. Some are only interested in a shallow approach. Others demand something with depth. As with adults, youth must be dealt with where they are right now emotionally, maturationally, spiritually, educationally. It is impossible to fit them all into a single program mold.

All leaders conclude that it is a mistake to center down in the spiritual life only, just as it is disasterous to engage in nothing but recreation. As one youth leader put it, "Kids may say they want to play all the time, but they don't. They're also looking for something serious, sometimes more than some adults." Youth, like adults, have needs for social involvement, for spiritual enrichment, for educational opportunities, and for Bible study. Offering any one of these to the exclusion of all others is like serving nothing but delicious fried chicken three times each day. Diners will soon be looking for another restaurant.

The most common mistake of inexperienced youth workers is to select one of the several different needs and say, "This is how you should do youth work. This is what youth should be interested in." So they load their program with that; then end up attracting only the youth who happen to have that particular kind of need, and losing out with the other three-fourths of kids whose needs are in one of the other pigeonholes.

"For where two or three are gathered in my name. . . ." (Matthew 18:20) gives us three keys to group work in the church, both adult and youth: (1) Two or three are necessary. Christian commitment maturity comes from meeting with others of like interest, not from a solitary pursuit of faith. (2) They must gather. It is not enough to occasionally run into each other. In many places, going to church on Sunday morning is not dissimilar from going to a movie on Saturday night. It may be inspiring, interesting, and mentally stimulating. But we have no relationship with the people who saw the show. So when it's over, we get up, go home, and forget it and them. Only in gathered communities do people find real strength and growth. (3) They must gather together in *his* name. Getting together isn't enough. Groups must be more than social, at least part of the time. For some people, conversion comes the day they join the church, instantly. For others, it comes more slowly, in bits and pieces. For most, unless Christian maturity through fellowship-acceptance is added to the new birth, "crib death" rises to a high percentage.

Many kinds of educational and group work systems are available through denominational publishing houses. But failure to have effective groups usually does not come from lack of good material. More often it arises from a lack of leadership in creating and structuring group life. The following outline says nothing about curriculum. But it has universal applications for starting and developing new adult groups:

1. It is usually easier to form new groups or classes than to add new people to the old ones.

2. Contact the couple in person (not by letter or phone) and invite them to join the new group. Paper never substitutes for the influence of personality.

3. Tell them the specific subject of the group (marriage problems, Bible study, raising children, or whatever).

4. Let them know that six to eight couples have been invited, and the group is limited to those who have been specifically invited. This makes the invitation personal. They have been selected.

5. Tell them that it will be casual with coffee (at least for those groups which meet in homes). Many folks won't show up in Sunday church school because of the rigid atmosphere.

6. Sunday morning in a home near the church can be an effective time and place for forming new groups. They have automatic babysitting with their children in church school. And it's hard to find an excuse not to come to something that happens on Sunday morning. There are very few time conflicts then.

7. Ask each couple to commit themselves to attendance every one of the eight weeks unless there is an emergency. This insures continuity and good discussions. It is also difficult for good group rapport to develop in less than six to eight weeks. It takes that many hours for people to trust each other.

8. Have a specific time span for the group, depending on what seems appropriate to the study. Six to eight weeks is best for a first group experience of new members or prospects. More than that sounds long.

9. Always meet in the same place at the same time. Don't drift from home to home at each meeting. People are creatures of habit about time and place. Drifting causes losses in attendance.

10. Have a specific leader or leaders for the entire study. Don't try to trade the teaching around in a group of new members. This runs shy and low self-confidence people away.

11. Tell them that the purpose is to give everyone an opportunity to get better acquainted and learn something at the same time. This lets them know the emphasis is on relationships rather than content. People have a greater felt need for getting acquainted than for getting informed.

12. Remember that one or two couples who have been inactive in the church can sometimes be reactivated by mixing them into new member groups. This is especially true if the subject matter is something in which they have personal interest. This also gives inactives a specific request for participation in something other than Sunday morning worship. Since they have been rejecting that for a long time, trying to plug them in somewhere else is more practical.

13. Be prepared for resistance by older members who have been working hard to make their Sunday school classes grow for years (without success). Help them to understand that people can be reached in this way who will never attend an established morning class.

An old farmer and his wife had been married for thirty years. One day the farmer's wife got a little worried. Not once during all those years had John told her he loved her. So when he came in from the field for dinner that day, she said to him, "John, why is it that you never do tell me that you love me?"

John replied crisply, "Woman, on the day I married you thirty years ago, I told you I loved you. So don't worry. If I ever change my mind, I'll tell you about it."

We say to new members on the day they join, "We're sure glad to have you." But do we find ways of saying it again? Do we find ways of helping them say it to each other? If not, we are probably losing many fine fish. This is one of those many places in life where once is not enough.

8

GOD'S QUARTERBACK

A quarterback does not do everything. But what he does is central to success. Unless he carries the ball effectively and passes it accurately, team progress becomes regress. What God's quarterback does with the ball is also the biggest single determiner of locker room mood. When statistics are stacked at year's end, they form a paper mirror of what he did in the crucial moments of his week.

His Personality:

What kind of person is he, this leader of a growing congregation? There is no one personality model. But he holds several qualities in common with others whose churches are having numerical growth. First of all and most of all, he is God's man. He is sold on the idea that Christ is *the answer* to the average human predicament. He likely knows the value of psychological counselling and does much of it. But that is not the brains of his message. Like Paul before him, his central vision is a man on a wooden cross. He preaches very little else because he knows little else works: Few people are pulled back from the brink of their respective disasters with the knotted end of a philosophical idea. Dudley Strain has observed, "He . . . brings with him human friendship . . . something more than is human—a knowledge of the truth which is their strength and shield."[1] The minister of a growing church is that kind of friend.

The three golden threads are incarnated in his life. His vertical relationship is rich and strong. The horizontal warmth is felt by every person he touches. He loves people in a thorough-going way that can never be missed or misconstrued. He actively seeks to lead people toward a relationship with Christ, not just to make the church grow, but because he knows it will supply the answer to their deepest needs. In doing this, he is not afraid to use words. He knows that the Word is more than just words. But he knows it frequently comes encased in words.

He aggressively experiments with all kinds of methods for drawing people close to Christ. Because of this wide-ranging activity, he often makes mistakes. He frequently looks back to "the methods we used last year," deploring his ignorance and lack of perspective. But such failures never drug him into lethargy. He can instantly describe two or three ideas "that we need to try as soon as we get time."

A laywoman in one growing church says, "I believe that Jim is God's man. I don't believe he's perfect. I don't have him on a pedestal. I see his humanness. But I believe that basically Jim wants what God wants for our church. He makes a lot of mistakes, and he admits his mistakes. But without a doubt, he is God's man. I think that's one of the reasons we're growing."

He is not necessarily a super-sophisticate. But one quality always stands tall enough to be instantly visible. He has the ability to relate to people on their level. He can accept them where they are, converse with them in a warm way, and seldom acts like a stuffed shirt. He leaves them with the gift of feeling worthwhile instead of a little stupid.

He knows that being available in the office is never a substitute for being available in the home. He is equally at ease in the Bible and on the sidewalk. He knows how to teach, but also how to listen. He knows how to preach, but also how to drink the fourteenth cup of coffee with words of appreciation. He knows how to manage a church, but also how to manage his own time so he can do the church's most important work. He knows that "No one can come to me unless the Father who sent me draws him. . . ." (John 6:44) But he also knows that Christ doesn't get as much done working alone as when he has help. He understands that people need to reach out and form warm relationships with others. But he also knows that many cannot reach out until the others reach out first. He always understands that family units are made up of individuals. So he never assumes that calling on the wife equals relating to the husband. He treats people as individuals, never as generalities.

If you dissected his private conversations and filed the fragments, most of them would stack up under five categories: (1) "I'm proud of you"; (2) "Tell me about yourself"; (3) "What is your opinion?" (4) An almost total refusal to find verbal fault with what another person thinks, says, or does; (5) Listening, listening, listening. The exceptions would follow those instances when he is asked for his opinion. In such cases he is direct and incisive, well able to express his viewpoints.

These five can most clearly be illustrated by thinking of their opposites, then reflecting on how frequently such conversations destroy grace relationship opportunities.

1. I'm proud of you. Opposites—"I'm not proud of you; Let me tell you what you did wrong; I'm proud of me; Let me tell you how great I am."

2. Tell me about yourself. Opposites—"I'm not interested in hearing about you; Let me tell you about me."

3. What is your opinion? Opposites—"Let me tell you about my opinion; Your opinion sounds a little stupid; I'm not really interested in your opinion."

4. Non-critical and non-judgmental statements. Opposites—Too numerous to print. While such verbal surgeries may be factually accurate, they murder relationships. Most people already have their inadequacies blueprinted. What they need is treatment, not diagnosis. And the most effective therapy is love-acceptance-grace in large doses.

5. Listen, listen, listen. Opposites—Eternal verbosity. But if the first four opposites are used, there will be little to listen to anyway. People seldom talk with people who won't listen.

His Convictions

It is not lack of skill that holds pastors back from growth leadership. Conviction comes first. Skill comes second. People seek and find the skill for evangelism, providing they have the will for it. A pastor who leads many evangelism workshops for other congregations reports that people often say to him, "I'd like to see our pastor get the kind of spirit which you have. We get excited about an evangelism idea, then go to the minister and he says, 'Well, you want to try it. Go ahead.' And kills it right there."

That pastor concludes that he would like to say to every local minister, "Do you see that evangelism is the first imperative in your ministry? You aren't going to lead anybody someplace where you aren't going."

The pastor of a growing church gives his attention to the biblical mission. Not to the exclusion of all others, but as his central and most important ministry. He is always seeking that one lost sheep as well as caring for the ninety-nine in the fold. Nor does he delude himself by thinking that evangelism mission will be done by osmosis if he nurtures people well.

A high school girl was getting instruction from a college senior on how to write themes. "First," he said, "you write the outline. Then you make your work fit around the outline." Leaders in growing churches are never confused about the central mission of the church. So they take that mission and make all other programatic aspects fit around it.

His Preaching

He is not necessarily a great orator. But his sermons epitomize the three virtues Paul prescribed for the church at Corinth. They are full of faith in a real God who acted for his people in history, and continues to act for them today. They are shot through with pellets of hope. They reiterate the need to love. The message content is high in biblical material, direct, and laced with applications to life on the street. He believes deeply in the church, but devotes very little pulpit energy to its preservation. He stands up on Sunday morning to proclaim a message, not to guard an institution.

His sermons have little of the "scare them out of hell" approach. On the contrary, they are coated more with grace than with fear. Nor do we find a limpid emotional preaching that tugs at the heartstrings while offending the intellect. His words are emotional, without feeling like soap-opera. They are intelligent, without sounding dictionary. They are forgiving, without advocating anarchy. They are judgmental without being hell-fire threats. They are spoken from the perspective of the prodigal's father. He didn't like pigpens, but he didn't waste time bad-mouthing them. He wanted his son to come home, but he didn't try to entice him by moving home closer to the pigpen.

T. R. Glover said, "I don't give tuppence for the man who goes in the pulpit to tell me where my duty lies; but I'll give all I have to the man who tells me whence my help comes."[2] The preacher we are describing does both, but you hear mostly the latter. A school principal in one growing church said, "I'm in a church that loves me and tells me that God loves me rather than saying, 'You're going to hell, and here's a way out.' There are not so many scare tactics here. Gene has brought a new message to our church. And the idea that God loves them seems kind of new to people."

Bonhoeffer asked the question, "Is it not possible that we cling too closely to our own favorite presentation of the gospel, and to a type of preaching which was all very well in its own time and place and for the social set-up for which it was originally intended?"[3] This may be one reason why charismatic churches have such an appeal to many people. Perhaps their message comes closer to the grace and hope that so many need to hear in this pressurized age.

A minister attended a David Wilkerson Crusade for youth in the high school auditorium. The message was utterly simple. It spoke of God's love and our need to repent of unlovingness. The pastor was astonished to see dozens of youth flooding onto the basketball floor in response to the super-simple message.

A pro football veteran stood before a man's breakfast. Lifting up two verses from Paul's pen, he spoke of the need to trust God one hundred percent for all your needs. Then he described his own experience at that point. A hush fell over the room as his truth penetrated the hectic swirl in each man's mind. You could hear a pin drop on the carpet. He had spoken to a need felt by everyone here—the need to stop trying to be our own God and start trusting in the real God. There was no dramatic oratory in his presentation. No super-illustrations embellished the point. He just told what Paul's idea had come to mean to him. But the power came through in a way seldom seen in church sanctuaries. He had passed the *word* to these men. It gripped their attention, and would likely change their life, at least for this day. Why? Because he spoke authentic message to authentic need.

We have seen that the medium is the message in evangelism. But the reverse is equally true, especially in the pulpit. The message is also the medium. It has a power all its own, completely apart from the fine prose in which it may come wrapped. No need to wonder if it has lost its punch in the missile age. We need only to ask whether we are faithful to the message Jesus preached. If we are, it will still get results.

Speaking to Pilot at his trial, Jesus said, ". . . For this I was born, and for this I have come into the world, to bear witness to the truth." (John 18:37) This is the preacher's task; not to speak his own message, but to bear witness to ultimate reality. Not to move people away from reality to a soft spiritualism; but to move them closer to the only reality. He doesn't have to depend on excitement dredged up from the morning paper, or on brain cells charged only with morning coffee. His message is God's message. So he doesn't begrudge time donated to sermon preparation. He knows people have a greater need for this product than for any they will buy at the corner drug store or supermarket.

All the cab drivers in a certain large city were given eye examinations by the department of public safety. Sixteen percent failed the exam. An official said, "We hate to create such a problem for the cab companies, but we still do have the old fashioned idea that cab drivers ought to be able to see where they are going." That difficult to define quality that some preachers have and some don't—the ability to see the essential nature of the gospel and how it applies to human personality—still stands high on the list of requirements for effective ministry. Without that, other methods will work some, but not enough.

His Administrative Leadership

A layman in one of America's fastest growing congregations says, "It all boils down to the minister. An energetic minister makes an energetic church. And he has to be dedicated to evangelism. That has to be one of his goals. I don't think it's something you can back into by accident. I don't think the congregation will rise up and say, 'Hey, let's get evangelistic.' Without the minister behind it, I don't think there would be a ground-swell movement to reach new people."

"When Jesus saw him and knew that he had been lying there for a long time, he said to him, 'Do you want to be healed?' " (John 5:6. A pastor must be prophet enough to ask this question in a tactful (but forceful) manner: "Do you really want to be healed of your non-growth?" Nothing else is likely to arrest the terminal narcissism that creeps into every successful church. If the pastor is unwilling to diplomatically kick a few cogs, it is unlikely that anyone else will correct this fatal drift.

Written in *Harpers Magazine* in December 1937, the following describes the administrative task of every pastor in timeless terms: "An idea originates with an individual. Because it came naturally from the depths of his experience, he sees it with great clarity. He is so much influenced by its power that he has to proclaim it. His high seriousness, his rapturous enthusiasm bring him disciples. They likewise must go out to show what they have found. But the idea is new and, therefore, to many people seems wrong. The disciples encounter apathy; they encounter overt enmity. In order that their idea may overwhelm all opposition they organize it. They must make the organization strong so that the idea may never be in danger. Developing such an organization requires endless attention. So they—or their followers, in turn—become so much occupied with the organizing that they forget the idea the organization was intended to perpetuate. The idea is gradually covered over with a smothering incrustation of all kinds of heavyweight machinery. Until some new life-giving individual comes along from within or without and shatters this incrustation and restores to the idea to its early state of free mobility, the organization is an enemy of the idea, instead of a guarantee of its life."[4]*

A congregation must first determine that it really does wish to go into all the world and make disciples (and not every church will want to). Some are like John Mark, who went home early from Paul's missionary journey. (Acts 13:13; 15:38) They would rather die quietly of arthritis than live on the edge of mission.

But most congregations really would like to grow. They are simply waiting for someone to tell them how. Listening conferences involving 33,618 laypersons and ministers from more than 250 congregations of the Christian Church (Disciples of Christ) were asked for their opinions about evangelism. They agreed on the following eight points:

1. There is a need for a concrete proposal/plan.
2. There is a need for a planned program of renewal.
3. There is a need for commitments of all persons in renewal/evangelism.
4. There is a need for motivation and developing of self-confidence.
5. No set model for renewal/evangelism will meet the needs of every congregation.
6. There is a concern for renewal/evangelism reaching persons rather than building numbers.
7. There is a need for providing help in setting goals and implementing them.
8. There is a need for leadership training in the area of renewal/evangelism.

It seems clear from this concensus that most churches want leadership help in evangelism. But where does the pastor start? He must begin with the church's key officers. Whether that be board, executive committee, cabinet, or elders; he must begin with the people who call the shots. A pastor cannot "grow" a church alone. This is always a corporate effort. So he must begin with the corporation officers.

He should start by calling their attention to the problem in clear graphic terms. Charts and graphs are helpful at this point. Sometimes he can both call their attention to the problem and begin to experiment with doing something about it at the same time. Some leaders are only willing to try something new after they have discussed the matter for a time. Other people only change their thinking after being involved in some action to help deal with the problem. So a both ways approach probably reaches the most people. If we don't discuss the problem, we won't be committed to solving it. But if we discuss it too long, we may become so depressed that action becomes impossible.

Once attention has been focused, the new methods must be implemented. "He said to them 'Cast the net on the right side of the boat, and you will find some.' . . . ." (John 21:6) What Jesus said applies to catching men as well. Some methods work; others don't. It is essential to find the one that works for our particular church in our particular community. Otherwise, we end up with frustration instead of fish.

The next ingredient our pastor will need is large doses of patience. "Jesus said to them, 'Follow me and I will make you become fishers of men.' " (Mark 1:17) He said he would *make them become.* That took a lot of time for Jesus—more than three years, plus a resurrection. So no pastor should expect the finished product of an outreaching, evangelistic church in three days, three Sundays, or three months. And sometimes it takes more than three years. So put Elmer's glue on your growth dream. It may not fly instantly.

Part IV

Being the Word

9

FIRST RUNG ON ANY LADDER

Flinging a flywheel into motion requires six times more energy than needed to keep it running afterward. Church growth momentum seems similar. When it's happening, it continues easily. But if growth is zero or negative, a reversal trend demands enormous effort. What if a pastor finds himself in a declining congregation? Assuming that he wants to ride the statistics the other direction (and not all pastors care that much), how can he get started?

He or she begins with faith. Without the faith that God wants evangelism done, and without the faith that he will help us do it, little happens. With it, anything can. God and methods do the work. But faith shifts the gears that set the methods in motion. A laywoman whose church has tripled in membership says, "You can't do God's work just by working. You have to believe. It seems like when we made up our minds to stop saying, 'We can't do this, and we can't do that,' and started saying, 'God will help us do it,' he did."

Abraham's family left Ur of the Chaldeans for a Promised Land they had never seen. How did they get there? By methods, of course. They packed their dishes. They folded their tents. They loaded their camels. They marched south. But it was Abraham's faith that propelled them into the methods. Without that, Canaan would have remained the impossible dream.

Moses marched his ragtag slaves out of Egypt with some methods in mind. They got strict instructions about what to pack, how to prepare for the trip. Their first stop would be the mountain of God. But the Hebrews were inspired to revolution by Moses' faith, not by his methods.

When Isaiah's generation headed west out of Babylon, what did they have to go on? Certainly not the facts. Jerusalem was a shambles, the temple destroyed, the government in ruins. But Isaiah's chapters forty thru fifty-five paint faith onto their despairing landscape. ". . . they shall run and not be weary, they shall walk and not faint." (Isaiah 40:31) These Jews didn't pack the moving vans because Isaiah showed them an urban renewal blueprint. They moved onto the desert trail behind a man of faith.

Church growth efforts involve a higher emotional risk than most other ventures. The failure of a small group program can easily be rationalized. When the Sunday school blows a flat, curriculum writers can shoulder the blame. But if people outreach falters, there is little protection from ego abrasion. "Maybe people just don't like us. Do you suppose we said the wrong thing?" And a dozen other condemnations rush to our head. So leadership begins with the communication of faith. Otherwise, people seldom risk trying any kind of method.

Faith can assuredly be pushed to ridiculous extremes. A young man believed he would one day become president of the U.S. He was always promoting a business scheme that should make a million. Every new idea was expected to cash out like Standard Oil did for Rockefeller. Did this young man have faith? No. He was suffering from delusions of grandeur, a psychiatric disturbance similar to astrodome construction on one square yard of real estate. But such illnesses are rare among church leaders. More often, they suffer from faith anemia. Until that is corrected, there is little energy available for any kind of evangelism method.

The faith needed for growth leadership goes far beyond self-confidence, positive thinking, or optimism (though all of these are helpful). Regardless of how skillful, personable, polished, gifted, or glib they may be, successful Word pushers know that self-faith is misplaced faith. We aren't that much by ourselves. So our hope must lie in what God can do in spite of our weaknesses.

The Bible advocates neither self-confidence nor delusions of grandeur. It calls for God-confidence. Listen to Paul and Barnabas drinking coffee at the Antioch Holiday Inn. What does Paul say? "I don't think there are many church prospects over in Asia Minor." No, that would be spiritual anemia. Nor does he say, "I can do all things." (delusion of grandeur) He says, "I can do all things in him who strengthens me." (Phillippians 4:13) That is a statement of faith.

Self-confidence is good, but not good enough. By itself it is like a car with three wheels. The three are essential, but insufficient. Paul writes, ". . . be strong—not in yourselves but in the Lord, in the power of his boundless strength." (Ephesians 6:10 Phillips) To the Corinthians he says, ". . . how serious was the trouble that came upon us in the province of Asia. . . . This was meant to teach us not to place reliance on ourselves, but on God. . . ." (II Corinthians 1:8-9 NEB).

A man named Smith has operated a drug store in a little New Mexico town for twelve years. During that time, seventeen ministers and countless laypersons trafficked his front door. All knew he was uninterested in religion. Smith is now a deacon, a tither, and a chairman of the stewardship committee. What happened? You can't define that. No one can say why people suddenly hear the *word* after a lifetime of deafness. But when someone had faith that God might do the impossible, they said, "We sure would be glad to have you come to church." During all those years of selling drugs to preachers, not one had ever tried to sell him on the church. When they finally did, the time was right in his life. So he decided to go.

An older couple lived in a small Texas town for twenty-five years. They never went to church; always attending fishing on Sunday mornings. He an Episcopalian, she a Catholic, they compromised and went no place. Now they are active church members and both hold elected offices. What happened? Someone believed that God might even do something new with people over forty. Several months later their new pastor asked if they had been offended by the church callers. "No," they replied. "Nobody from any church has called on us in more than fourteen years. We were impressed that someone cared about us that much."

In a small Oklahoma town, a man in his mid-thirties had attended church as a youth. Then he lost touch. Now he has reaffirmed his faith and serves as the youngest elder in that congregation. Why? Someone had enough faith to think God might not be finished with John yet. So they invited him to church. All word outreach starts thusly. Methods are seldom applied until we begin to have faith in the power of God.

The cynical writer of Ecclesiastes said, "What is crooked cannot be made straight. . . ." (Ecclesiastes 1:15) Contrast that to the last chapters of the New Testament. ". . . Behold I make all things new. . . ." (Revelation 21:5) The pessimist of Ecclesiastes had faith in himself, and it led him to cynicism. The writer of Revelation had faith in God, and it led him to gold plated optimism. "Don't give up on anyone; God can do what you cannot," is the trademark of New Testament leaders. If not yet equipped with that attitude, go back to start. Pray until you have it. All success begins here.

After effective methods are started and growth begins, the temptation increases to rely on methods alone. A racehorse enthusiast tells about an inexperienced jockey riding in his first race. Unfortunately, his horse got off to a bad start leaving the gate. In fact, she fell down. As the jockey picked himself up off the ground he prayed, "Lord, this sure is embarrassing, but if you'll help that horse to get up, I'll get on and we can still run the race."

The horse got up, the jockey scrambled on, and off they went. Since they were now far behind the other horses, he prayed again. "Lord, if you'll just help this horse to catch up a little, I sure would appreciate it."

Sure enough, his horse began to close the gap. But when he caught up with the group, they were so tightly packed that he couldn't get through. So he prayed again. "Lord, if you'll just open up a hole so we can get through, it sure would help."

A hole appeared and he went right through. Now they were coming down the backstretch. He was out in front. You know what he prayed then? "I believe I can handle this myself now, Lord. Get up and run you son of a gun."

This inclination to feel self-sufficient is a zerox of Adam's error. Overcome by the urge to become their own god, he and Eve had their lease terminated early. "That won't work," their Landlord was saying. "Whenever you try to live without me, you get booted out of your personal paradise." The same with church growth. Without faith, it is not created. It continues in faith. Whenever that factor fades from consciousness, our success story falls apart.

A traveling salesman stopped to see a friend. The conversation revealed that he was in a selling slump, hadn't sold much for about a month. Really down, he was questioning his ability and himself. He might even quit the company.

The following month he stopped by again. "How are sales going?" the friend inquired over a cup of coffee. "The last time we talked, you were sure blue."

"Oh, things are going great," he replied. "I've had an exceptional month."

"How did you ever solve your problem?" the friend asked. "Did you find out what you were doing wrong?"

"I decided that my real problem was my faith," he said with a smile. "So I finally prayed and turned it all over to God. After that, things began to get better. Maybe I needed reminding that regardless of how good a salesman I am, I just don't have control of everything."

God does expect us to pass the word. That takes methods. But he doesn't expect our brilliance to be a substitute for the word. Paul's theology applies to whole churches as well as to individuals: "For by grace you have been saved through faith; . . . not because of works, lest

65

any man should boast." (Ephesians 2:8-9)

After Jesus raised a ruler's daughter from death, two blind men asked him for healing.

"Do you believe that I am able to do this?" he asked.

"Yes, Lord," they replied.

Then he touched their eyes. "According to your faith be it done to you," he said. (Matthew 9:27-29)

Word miracles begin there too. Methods move muscles, systems, people, and paper. That is needed. But faith moves mountains. When trying to start a parked church, you begin with faith.

10

SOLD ON THE PRODUCT

This fellow stumbled into my office. Visibly under the influence, he smelled terrible. "You are the only thing between me and suicide," he said. "I'm drunk. I've lost my job. I've lost all self-respect. I've lost my family. I have nothing left to live for."

So I befriended him and let him talk awhile. Several hours later he was sober enough to listen. The next day I went with him to an AA meeting. That first night he committed himself to Alcoholics Anonymous and sobriety. In the more than twenty-two years since then, he has never departed from it. Over the years you could just see the spiritual growth. Like regular church attendance—he never misses, always sits in the same place. He is now one of the largest contributors in our congregation. Considering that we have more than four hundred giving units, that's pretty good.

But the greatest part of the story is the way he is always out helping people. "Look, I have been where you are," he will say. "I know somebody who can help you." He usually doesn't try to get the message across himself. His approach is to get the guy into my office. He always brings each one in personally. When they arrive he says to me in a rough sort of way, "Now I want you to hit this fellow right between the eyes, just like you did me."

This guy has brought in a constant procession of people across the years. And I have sent many to him. If a really bad alcoholic comes in, I call him. He'll drop everything and come. To him, alcoholism is an experience that nobody needs to hold onto. I have heard him say to so many people in AA meetings, "That's a good step, but it's just one step. You really need to get your life right. And I'm going to take you to a man who will tell you about that." And he does.

This page from a Florida pastor's mental diary illustrates another essential foundation block. Word passing roots out of the spiritual experiences of congregational leaders. People not sold on the product themselves are unlikely to work at giving it to others.

As I remember after hearing one of Dr. Abraham Maslow's tapes, all people have four basic needs: (1) the need for security; (2) the need for love, affection, and a sense of belonging; (3) the need for recognition and esteem; and (4) the need for new experiences. Churches can certainly help meet these. But the Word meets a more comprehensive need that underlies them all: the need to decide on that to which we will give the ultimate concern of our personality. Unless that need is met in a positive way, whole "personhood" eternally eludes us. And unless we have personally experienced the meeting of that ultimate need, we cannot fully understand its immense value for others.

One pastor described a conversation with a man who is highly active in several social and fraternal organizations: "His calendar is so full that he hardly has time to breathe because of his philanthropic involvements. Two long-distance calls on such matters came while we sat there in his living room talking. But he said to me, 'I've got all this fellowship. I'm active in Scouts. I'm active in Masons. But there's still something missing in my life. I can't put my finger on it, but I know it's there. And I want it.' I sat there thinking while he was answering the phone again, 'What you are yearning for is not more relationships with people; you are seeking a deeper relationship with God.' "

The pastor has learned what many have not been able to grasp, especially in these last two scientifically saturated decades: People find through the church something they cannot find anywhere else in society. When such a conviction runs in the mental circuits of leaders, they tend to look for methods that will help people find what they are seeking. If this perception is absent, they are poorly motivated toward people outreach.

If a salesman isn't sold on his product, he isn't likely to sell much of it. Word passing is not selling: it's more like one stalled motorist telling another where to get gas. But the motivational principle is similar.

68

Large black letters above a storefront in Lubbock, Texas, shout, "Human Development Center." But the great glass eyes of the building are stark naked. The occupants who hung the sign have either moved elsewhere or shut down the project. Driving on west toward the university, one passes various buildings with denominational names out front. Erected by dedicated Christians in decades past, they too are centers for human development.

Since their fronts do not have picture windows, it is impossible to tell whether they are vacant or occupied. But a careful investigation would likely determine that many of their occupants have also moved elsewhere. If not physically, then mentally. Some have become professional bureaucrats who seldom leave the office except to call in the hospital. Others, casualties of the fragmented sixties, have dropped out altogether. Still others remain through a lifetime of meetings which puzzle over "why nothing is happening in our church."

Numerous theories can be listed for this lost focus concerning the mission of the church. But shovel off the layers of rationalization and you will find just plain old doubt—doubt that the word which this organization promotes is worth that much to anybody. As long as this doubt remains, no number of leadership seminars on evangelism will turn the statistical slide uphill.

Do we want the growth success of the early apostles? Then we shall need to return to their basic ideas: (1) Christ has a word of notable value for every human being; (2) This word is more important than anything they have yet heard; (3) All obstacles must be overcome in delivering it.

Paul was convinced of the gospel's value. When we get that convinced, we will have similar results. If we don't understand that our message is *the Message*—if we don't see that it can bind up the raveled ends of our frustrated humanness—then we will keep it in the reserved section of our pew libraries. If we see the word as Paul saw the word, we will likely thrust it into circulation.

A newspaper reporter scratching for a New Year's story interviewed all the pastors in a small town. He asked each one what important thing had happened in their church during the past year. One minister said their most significant achievement was putting in a new sidewalk and some shrubbery. When a church works from this priority view, growth is approximately as likely as raising geraniums in the concrete sidewalk.

The pulpit committee in another church suggested that they offer a ten dollar raise for every new member the pastor could recruit. That is a slight variation on the more common theme of seeking new members to help pay the building payments. While both sound practical, neither is effective. Both begin from a posture of selfishness. Church growth seldom flourishes in such soil.

Jesus put a condition on the Apostles' evangelism ability. "But you shall receive power *when* the Holy Spirit has come upon you; and you shall be my witnesses. . . ." (Acts 1:8) The same is still true. Whatever our methods, only the power of God's Spirit working in us can do his work. Evangelism therefore begins with worship. If our seeking is sincere, God will give wings to the feeble methods we devise or expropriate from others.

If our quest for church growth is not authentic (motivated by the urge to help people find God), our work will be not long blessed. Early successes have been experienced by some churches who seek new members in order to pay the mortgage, raise the status of the church in the community, or up the ego of a ladder climbing pastor. But members quickly tire of doing good things for the wrong reasons. So the early fruit that holds such promise often catches a killing frost in the April of its progress.

The first step in many congregations is to sit down together and ask: (1) Why are we here? (2) In the light of why we are here, what had we ought to be doing? (3) In light of what we ought to be doing, what are some methods by which we might accomplish such doings? If the Word is solidly present in parish personalities, these hard questions are usually asked. When answered with thoughtfulness, prayer, and action, numerical growth is a likely result.

11

HITCH YOUR WAGON TO THE SPIRIT

The strong emphasis on prayer found in most growing churches takes many different forms. Some pray daily for the goal of winning a specific number of new members each year. Others pray for the specific persons on whom they are calling each week. Many do both. Many have strong patterns of group prayer by elders and other church leaders who are responsible for growth. Still others have found value in the "prayer partner" idea which seems to radically improve attitudes and flow of concern for each other as well as those outside the ranks. No small ingredient in any of these forms is the pastor's leadership. He appears to verbalize the value of prayer in teaching and preaching at a higher level than is generally found in churches of lesser growth.

Whatever format it takes, the practice of prayer by many members obviously increases the vertical connection with God (thus strengthening the *being* thread of our analogy). When people pray, many fringe benefits are added to the cake mix of congregational life. Members become more sensitive to the needs of people around them; more sensitive to God's will (which certainly includes reaching people outside the church); and more able to communicate with prospects in an effective, accepting manner. As a great physician, Alexis Carrell, has observed, "If you make a habit of sincere prayer, your life will be very noticeably and profoundly altered. Prayer stamps with its indelible mark our actions and demeanor. A tranquility of bearing, a facial and bodily repose, are observed in those whose inner lives are thus enriched."[1]

Jesus told his disciples, " . . . he who believes in me will also do the works that I do; and greater works than these will he do. . . ." (John 14:12) Why do we not seem to collect on that astonishing promise? One of the biggest reasons is because we don't pray like he did. Growing churches do much more than just pray. But the practice of prayer, individually, and especially in groups, is obviously a powerful channel through which God can move to get his word across.

The student work director was giving his guest speaker a tour of the campus ministry building. As they walked down a hallway, the guest saw a sign marked "prayer room" over a doorway. As they moved past, it became obvious that the director didn't intend to show him that room. Curious, he reached for the knob. His nostrils were assaulted by a musty smell. The room was stuffed with boxes, boots, clothes hangers, and junk. On the little altar stood a pair of worn cowboy boots, an old Gilby's Vodka box, and a roll of toilet tissue. A bit embarrassed, the director explained quickly, "We used this for a storage room during the summer. Just haven't gotten it cleaned out yet."

At first it seemed like a sacrilegious thing to the visitor—stacking a prayer room full of junk. But then he realized that the room was a parable of his own life. So busy traveling around the country speaking and doing good things, he had lost the habit of praying. The time he had formerly spent talking with God each day was now crowded full of other things.

Look at the biography of Christ again. What characteristic of his life-style makes him different from other persons? One of the most obvious is his praying. Many times the disciples would awaken early in the morning to discover Jesus missing from the camp. They found him out by himself, praying. In the midst of great crowds clamoring for his healing touch, he often withdrew into a quiet place to pray. If Jesus needed to do that, how can you and I expect to live effectively without it? And how can churches hope to succeed without it?

And yet we try. If we pray, it is usually because of a personal crisis—like the man who said he prayed the most serious prayer of his life standing on his head. Someone asked him why he did it upside-down. Was he into yoga or something? "No, I fell into an old well, and it was the only thing I could do." Even when we pray in church, it is often out of habit, like when we zip and unzip meetings.

Do you remember what the eleven remaining Apostles did after Jesus' final ascension? They went back to Jerusalem and waited in prayer for God to give them directions. How different from what we would probably do. We would likely go back to the city and wait for a committee to be appointed. We would wait for a religious survey to be conducted, evaluating the religious needs of modern man. Or wait for a new minister to be called, so he could come and solve all our problems.

But the disciples had sense enough to wait for the right thing in the right way. Because they did, the day of Pentecost came. It didn't happen instantly. They didn't have a sixty minute service and walk out with all the answers. Fifty days passed before the Holy Spirit gave them insight, a sense of direction, and power. But because they waited in the right way, it did come.

An evening speaker stayed overnight in a small Texas community. He rose early the next morning to attack a briefcase full of work before catching his next plane. Working at the desk in his guest bedroom, he found himself without an eraser. Cautiously opening the desk drawer, he hoped to find one there. He found something better. Laying on top of some papers was a little business card. Its printed words became the word to his exhausted brain. "Prayer is the pulse of the renewed soul; and the constancy of its beat is the best test and measure of the spiritual life." And that day he went back to a habit he had lost in the shuffle of his "busyness."

You can always estimate a person's spiritual depth by the breadth of their praying. If they aren't doing much praying, you won't find God doing much in their life. The same is true of congregations. God won't work any miracles where people won't let him. And prayer is the primary tool by which he gets miracles done. Someone asked E. Stanley Jones for the secret of his tremendous physical energy. He wrote more than two dozen books and preached three times a day across India, China, and America. This went on for more than forty years. He replied, "I have kept up my prayer life daily. So I do not face life alone."[2]

We celebrate Pentecost each June and completely miss its point. The big news about Pentecost does not concern the Holy Spirit coming to the Apostles. The big message of Pentecost is that God can still do this for people. He can still get his word across to us. Like some gigantic radio station filling the airwaves of the world, he is reaching out for his children every second. If we are receptive to that word by tuning our minds to his mind through prayer, he can still give us insights, a sense of direction, and power.

Evangelism success in the New Testament is a result of people receiving the Holy Spirit. It isn't something they did just by working at it. Jesus told his disciples, "But you shall receive power when the Holy Spirit has come upon you; and you shall be my witnesses in

Jerusalem and in all Judea and Samaria and to the end of the earth."
(Acts 1:8) And how did they get the Holy Spirit? By prayer. When
Jesus said, " . . . Ask, and it will be given you. . . ." (Luke 11:9); Huck
Finn thought he was talking about things like a new fishing rod. But
Jesus is speaking here of the Holy Spirit. "If you . . . know how to give
good gifts to your children, how much more will the heavenly Father
give the Holy Spirit to those who ask him!" (Luke 11:13) Why don't
we receive this today? Usually because we don't ask, either as individuals or as congregations.

Even if we are convinced that prayer is important, there is always
the time crunch. "I'm so busy. How can I find the time?" But perhaps
we are putting the question the wrong way. Suppose a friend said, "If
you will get up fifteen minutes earlier every morning for the next
several days, I'll send someone over to your house during that time.
When you go to answer your doorbell, he'll hand you a crisp new twenty dollar bill."

What would you say? "I just don't have time. I just can't get up that
early." It is equally ridiculous to say we don't have time to pray. The
real question is, "Can we afford not to pray? With this kind of power,
insight, and direction available through this source—free—can we afford not to accept it?" If we really believe the Spirit of God is real, we
will have less trouble finding time to pray. Our crisis is not so much
one of time as of belief—belief that God is real and that Pentecost is a
potentially contemporary event.

If we do decide to take prayer seriously, there are several simple
things to remember. First, follow the pattern of Jesus. Do it alone.
Jesus did pray in other ways. He prayed before eating. He prayed in a
retreat with the whole group. He prayed at the time of his baptism. He
prayed with three close friends. He prayed on the cross. And the early
disciples prayed in other ways too. They prayed in the temple. They
prayed as a group in the upper room. They prayed in homes. They
prayed at meals. They prayed in jail. They prayed on housetops. They
prayed when they were alone and when they were together.

But the method Jesus consistently used to get his personal direction
and power was alone. Giving the disciples instruction in prayer, he
says, " . . . go into your room and shut the door and pray to your
Father who is in secret. . . ." (Matthew 6:6) God is not likely to talk
with you in a crowd, or over spilled rice crispies and chattering
children. Nor will he chase you down in the cabbage section of a supermarket, tap you on the shoulder and say, "May I have a word with
you?" Perhaps occasionally, but not often.

If you are not accustomed to praying, it is hard to begin. Your mind
is instantly full of distracting thoughts—the dress you are making, the
job on your desk for Monday morning, the car payment. Will power
alone is never sufficient to still a whirring brain. Many people find
that reading a chapter in the Bible is a good way to clean their mind of
distracting thoughts. Some find it helpful to pray a specific one-line

74

prayer five times over. Some samples of these are: Lord Jesus Christ, fill me with your presence for this one moment. Lord Jesus Christ, have mercy on me. Lord Jesus Christ, help me to abide in you.

Next, pray for three people you know who need God's help today. By this time you have started taking your mind off yourself and putting it on God. It is hard to think of self and pray for someone else simultaneously. Then think of that person you hate more than anyone else in the world—that person who consistently drives you up the wall. Pray for them. By this time, your mind is producing mostly alpha waves. This is the electronically measurable state of mind in which God best communicates with people.

Before you stop, be sure to spend some time listening. Relax all your muscles after praying a few minutes, and just listen. When you try to converse with some people, it's hard to say anything. They're too busy talking. God may feel the same about some of our conversations with him. Try praying for creative ideas, then listening in the silence for things God may say to you. You may want to keep a notebook of what you hear. Try writing down two things that you personally could do to help your church grow. Try writing down the names of three persons you ought to contact for the church.

Don't stop too soon. Prayer must be learned, and most people must pray ten minutes a day for several consecutive days before they experience the sense of God's presence. Many report after two days, "Nothing, it just doesn't work for me." In a few more days they come back and say, "Now I understand what you mean. It finally happened. I wish I had learned that a lot earlier in my life." You don't learn to ride a bicycle in one day. And the disciples waited fifty days for God, so don't stop too soon. He will come to you if you wait for him.

Many find a prayer card helpful in focusing their concentration. A few mental hooks may be written on the card to serve as reminders. The following are samples of such words: *Thanksgiving:* Focusing the mind on things for which you are thankful today helps clean the garbage out of your emotional system. God's Spirit has trouble getting into an organism filled with pessimism, gloom, and self-sympathy; *Three Church Members:* Pray for three people you feel need God's help today; *Pastor:* That God will strengthen him; *One Enemy:* Don't pray that you can love him. That may be impossible. Pray that God can love him through you; *Insight:* Into yourself, and for the solution to your problem; *Witness:* Pray that God will lead you to one person today who you can invite to church.

The next big problem is how to keep on praying. Even after you discover its power, the habit is hard to hang on to. There are so many distractions. A few days of business trip during which we miss praying, and the habit has evaporated. How can we crowd out the things that keep crowding God out?

A young pastor became involved in a prayer covenant with his elders. Under pressure of great problems in the church—financial and numerical—the men had tried everything else, so they decided to pray. Each made an agreement that they would pray for all the others by name, every day. They would pray for insights into the problems of the church. They would pray for three members of the church each day. Once a week they would gather for an hour to discuss a chapter they had read in Timothy, and find out how the experiment was going.

By the end of two weeks, amazing things were happening. Old animosities had healed over. They were reporting peaceful minds in spite of life stresses. Within a few weeks, the church's financial problems disappeared. The young minister learned though this experience the nature and power of praying. His promise to the other group members kept him praying long enough so that he finally experienced the reality of God.

A similar approach is essential in most congregations. Praying churches don't happen by accident. Unless we in some way band together to hold each other to our best, we find it hard to begin and keep the discipline. A belief in the power of praying is the key to *starting*. But drawing strength from others is the key to continuing. A good approach is to challenge church school classes, elders, the evangelism committee, or other natural groups to make a serious prayer covenant for thirty days. Rather than forming special prayer groups, it is more practical to use the natural structures within the congregation. This engages key leaders in prayer, rather than a few people who are already sold on it.

A denominational executive was sitting in the Albuquerque airport waiting on his flight. Drinking a cup of coffee, he was killing time by reading a book. His concentration was gradually disrupted by the conversation between a waitress and the man sitting at his elbow. Obviously old acquaintances, she was telling him about her recent trip to Japan. After several minutes of this instant travelogue (which overseas tourists trot out at the least provocation), she concluded by saying, "It was wonderful, but I sure am glad to be home. You know, if you don't speak the language, it's really hard."

That overheard sentence stuck in his mind like a spear flung from God. "If you don't speak the language, it's really hard." That's the way it is. Prayer is the language by which we speak with God. More important, by which he speaks with us. If we don't speak the language, it's really hard for him to get across to us. How about you? Do you speak the language?

Part V

Overcoming Theological Hang-ups

12

GOD OR METHODS?

For many, the old paradox between the power of God and the power of methods is a mental block to every sane discussion of church growth. "Nothing we can do will make a church grow," one man said. "Only God can add to the church."

That is true. And because our study concentrates so hard on church growth *methods,* it is necessary to say firmly that church growth does not come from methods. Evangelism is not something we do; it is something God does through us. And the method he uses to get it done through us is his word. Without that, no kinds of human methods will be adequate.

"Pray as if it all depends on God. Work as if it all depends on you," advises another old paradox. Equally true in evangelism. Only God accomplishes the drawing of new persons to himself. New life in Christ is not something we manufacture in church plant assembly lines. On the other hand, evangelism never flies without methods. The way by which church people try to influence non-church people toward Christ can be classified under various kinds of *methods.* Without such methods God would have a hard time getting his word through to people.

"Which comes first, the chicken or the egg?" asks another ancient paradox. Actually, both come first. The egg is potential within the chicken. The chicken is potential within the egg. On the other hand, neither comes first. It is always God who comes first. He gives the power for life to both chicken and egg. "In the beginning, God. . . ." (Genesis 1:1) is likewise the answer to evangelism's God/method paradox.

In a too crude analogy, the gasoline that powers evangelism is the word of God. Methods are the motor into which the gasoline is poured as God's people try to move others toward Christ. Both the motor and the gasoline are essential to the process. In a sense, both come first. But it is always God who gives life and power to the system.

What is this word God uses to power church growth? An exact definition is impossible. We can never draw a precise circle around God and his activity. If we could, he would not be God; we would be his God. Then, too, even the Bible uses *word* several different ways. For the apostle John, the Word is Christ. When he uses Word (Logos) in the first chapter of his Gospel, he means the super-rational, extra-normal person intervention of God into the personal experiences of "personkind." In other parts of the New Testament, word means the message which Christ preached, the words and good news of grace that he brought from God. In the Old Testament, word covered a diversity all the way from God making Adam out of mud; to broadcasting his will through Moses, the lawgiver; and predicting the future through Isaiah, the prophet. His word is also seen in historical interventions like manna in the desert and the Poor Richard type wisdom of Proverbs.

Our contemporary *word* includes all these meanings, plus richness indescribable. It is that life changing, life redirecting force which God sent into the world in Christ. Through this means God saves his people from themselves and from those demonic secret agents (whether personified with pitchforks or not) which subvert our lives in all the wrong directions.

When the Word (Christ) is truly communicated to a person, faith becomes a possibility, whereas it may never have been an option before. Such an experience lifts human existence away from littleness and emptiness toward greatness in God. No wonder the Bible describes word so many different ways. It is always new and different each time it comes, because it is the present act of God's revelation to a unique person.

Some say the word comes primarily through scripture. Others see the Word exploding out of the Holy Spirit's ministry. A few describe it as God's revelation to persons through presently understood celestial communication (para-psychological perhaps). Still others feel that the *word* comes primarily through words preached

78

from a pulpit. Its interaction can be (and has endlessly been) described using the technical jargon of psychology, learning theory, sociology, spiritualism, religious experience, and cultural growth. Some people, like the Greeks, would describe it as insight and reason. Others, like the Jews, would call it power. Still others would term it a new sense of direction.

But none of these cerebral systems totally define the Word (even exhaustive efforts like that of Paul Tillich). Each is too limiting if used alone. The redeeming hand of God, seen so vividly in Jesus Christ, comes to human beings at various times in various places in various ways. It is one of those things (like romantic love) which must be experienced firsthand before we can be sure it exists. Even then we have only a vague awareness of its definition.

Conversion is the most commonly used term to describe the Word's impact on personality. And it's a good word still, regardless of its linguistic tarnish. But even that description is never comprehensive enough to describe what happens when God's Christ meets God's child on some unexpected Damascus road and turns his life downside-up. So no claim is made here to an exhaustive definition of how God uses Word to intersect the tangents of our lives. We simply assert three things from the observation of human experience and behavior: (1) The Word has come into the world; (2) It continues to come into the minds of new persons in this generation; (3) It is a life-transforming force to which nothing can be compared in intensity and redeeming possibility.

A man got up early one morning to leave for a trip. The house was dead dark. Stumbling across the room, he found his glasses and fumbled them on. They were good lenses, ground to precision and properly fitted by a good optometrist. The molded prisms allowed him to see slightly better than before. But not until he flipped the light switch was his visibility significantly better.

"Personkind" has knowledge and is piling it in larger stacks every year. We have better methods for everything. These can be learned and improved upon. But when the Word comes to personality, it does more than educate. It does more than acculturate. It does more than motivate. It illuminates life in a way that nothing else can, in a way that suddenly "makes all things new" instead of just better.

This God-person transaction is the goal towards which all the methods in these pages seek to point people. The techniques should not be construed as means for making churches bigger. That would be insufficient reason for both writing a book and reading it. Nor should it be thought that any kind of method can take control of the light switch for anyone. That matter is always between the person and God.

But are there ways we can encourage more people to begin looking for the switch? Do certain principles underlie all the various methods for getting people to reach for it? The answer is yes.

13

MIRAGES GET IN
OUR EYES

A half dozen Easterners were on their way to the California gold
fields in 1849. Crossing the Llano Estacado (staked plains) in what is
now southeastern New Mexico, they ran out of water. One thirsty day
passed. Still no streams were in sight. They doggedly followed the
faint desert trail into the second day. Shortly after noon, one man
sighted a bright green burst of trees off to the right. Behind them
glimmered a pool of blue water.

Excited, the group rode like fury in that direction. But when their
horses topped the last rise, the beautiful view evaporated.Thirty miles
of dry mesquite bush and sand spread before them. Starting back
toward the trail, their attention was again arrested by a pool of water
in the distance. Result: repeat performance of the first hopeful ride.

One day later a cavalry patrol came across the lone survivor. The
others had perished, their mucous membranes cooked to parchment in

80

the Southwest sun. Only two miles away the water hole had vainly awaited their arrival. It was squarely on the trail they had abandoned to chase mirages.

Church growth hopefuls often follow similar disaster patterns. It isn't that congregations have no inclination to grow. It isn't that preachers have lost interest in motivating people to faith in Christ. More often, a shimmering mirage that looks like truth has led them off in what looked like a good direction.

Before we try to recognize our current mirages, it may be helpful to identify some from the recent past. They are always easier to see than those of the present. Some sort of pietism was probably the chracteristic mirage type during the early part of this century. Versions of this included everything from theological fundamentalism to the ill-fated temperance movement that briefly "paused" the booze market during the 1930s. In the booming fifties, a main mirage was the "cheap grace" method of dragging into membership any sheep who would sign a card. During that time many also drew false hopes from the blossoming ecumenical movement. In the sixties it was often the cry for social reform that drew us off the trail. Each of these was supposed to produce a Christian world in a hurry. One even promised to do it in one generation.

History has not yet provided appropriate distance for a complete cataloging of today's mirages. So labeling attempts will likely be more general than definitive. But perhaps we can see enough of them to send us Sherlock Holmesing after others not quite so obvious.

The Love Your Neighbor Mirage: Robert Raines said in his excellent book *Reshaping the Christian Life,* "A servant people inevitably becomes a witnessing community."[1] While that sounded like a keystone for evangelism theology in 1964, the light of history shows its inadequacy as a general truth. Congregations who pride themselves on many acts of Christian love toward people in their community do not always move on to become great evangelistic churches. In fact, many of them have maintained a zero population escalation for ten years. When it is pointed out that their doing witness alone doesn't carry the day, they generally insist that it still will. They just need to work a little harder and a little longer.

Total reliance on doing is no more adequate than the total reliance on being (pietism) of earlier decades. So file that mirage under trash too. Jesus did urge his disciples to practice spiritual disciplines like prayer, disciplines that would lead them to a deepening love for God. Today we might call that pietism. And he told them to love their neighbors, even the despised Samaritan outcast, and sent them out to heal people. That is similar to our recent outcry for social justice. But he added one more thread. He told them to verbally persuade others to test these practices in their own life. Had he not, his gospel message would likely have died with that first generation of Galilean fishermen, tax collectors, prostitutes, and peasants.

81

Acts is the history of growing churches which applied all three golden threads. They met together daily for prayer—being the Word. They cared for the needy, shared their food together gladly, and reached into every strata of society without prejudice—doing the Word. But the record is also loaded with verbal proclamations to groups, families, and individuals—saying the Word. When Paul wrote, "For I am not ashamed of the gospel. . . ." (Romans 1:16) he was obviously talking about its vocal distribution, not just its social implications or spiritual aspects.

The Intellectual Good Works Mirage: "If we could just get our Christian education program upgraded, maybe our church would grow."

"If we could just improve our church school curriculum. . . ."

"If we could just get people to hold the correct doctrinal beliefs. . . ."

"If people would just believe the right biblical interpretations. . . ."

"If we could just teach people to have the right theology about God. . . ."

Whatever variation such convictions take, they are actually a thinly varnished form of Gnosticism, the heresy of the early church which asserted that we are saved by "right thinking." Wherever Christians begin to think that a certain type of intellectual belief is *the* religious answer, that idea subtly usurps the role of God in that congregation, denomination, or group. This sophisticated form of idol worship prevents the worship of God—not by suggesting that its adherents take up atheism (which almost never works in America); but by substitution of a new god (which almost always works anytime, anywhere).

Though hard to tell apart when inside your head, intellectual faith and authentic faith are radically different. Intellectual faith is the belief that God may help you if you can just think and act in the proper way (the kind of faith the Pharisees had). Authentic faith is the belief that God *will* help you if you make the leap of faith in his direction (the kind of faith the early Christians had). Intellectual faith can be a life enriching force, and has been for many. But authentic faith goes beyond enrichment; it is a life changing and empowering force. And this is what most people are looking for in a religious experience; not just intellectual enrichment but life changing empowerment.

The Christian Education Mirage: "If we concentrate on helping Christians to grow in Christ, they will automatically attract other people and the church will grow."

However you describe the two great tasks of the church—converting and educating, or birthing and maturing—each pole deserves equal attention. No congregation does the whole work of the gospel by limiting itself to one or the other. Working only at the education-maturity-nurture role would equal the twelve apostles nailing up the doors of their Jerusalem church so that they could devote total energy to helping Thomas overcome his doubts and Peter get over his impulsive bullheadedness.

On the other hand, devoting total time to reaching the unchurched would be like filling a great hospital with competent physicians in the field of delivering babies, then having nobody on the pediatric floor to care for them after you get them born. Birth and health care: both are equal necessities. One without the other will eventually extinguish both hospitals and churches.

The Personal Responsibility Mirage: "They know where the church is. Why should we need to go out and try to convince them to come to it? People have to take some responsibility for themselves, don't they?"

That sounds like a rational protest against pavement pounding and door knocking. But flip back to Jesus' parable of one hundred sheep. Ninety-nine are safely home in bed, but one is out fooling around in the bushes. The story shows that God cares about all the sheep, but his preeminent concern at that moment is for the AWOL one.

That doesn't mean we should center all church activity around one sheep out in the brush. Such programming would keep us on a permanent bivouac while the other ninety-nine are left neglected at home (without food and water). The same Christ who said, "Go into all the world," also said, " . . . Feed my sheep." (John 21:17) So his modern disciples must also seek a balance between looking for lost lambs and tending the flock.

But few modern congregations need reminders to come home and feed those safe in the pen. Very rarely do we find a church that has overloaded in the direction of evangelistic mission. Their more common danger comes from officers and leaders complaining about too much effort spent on a few unappreciative lambs.

A protest against lack of program balance would be valid, if accurate. But complaints about lack of appreciation are totally inappropriate. Jesus' parable says nothing at all about a need for the lamb to show appreciation to the shepherd. Nor do we find the sheep calling on the phone with a plea for paramedics. The story doesn't even tell us whether the sheep *knows* he is lost. It just says that he is not at home. Not finding him (her?) in the pen forms sufficient cause for the shepherd to pull on his hiking boots.

A similar motivation impels God's asphalt sheep herders into today's neon wilderness. The decision about whether to go or not go has nothing to do with whether the lost have telegramed a willingness to take responsibility for themselves. Nor does it require that they appreciate the scouts who look for them. We go because God sends us, not because the sheep submit a petition for spiritual assistance.

The Goal Setting Mirage: A recent fad calls for the congregation to set long range goals. This magic procedure is supposed to produce a high degree of involvement, personal commitment, and warm fuzzy feelings for the church. These virtues are great and valid. And most churches under-apply goal techniques rather than overwork them. But concentration on goal setting can also be a side track. Whatever goals we hold firmly in mind over a period of months or years, we are very likely to achieve. Unfortunately, these may be the *only* goals we reach.

Far more important than goal setting is the need to pick the *right* goals to set. Look again at the three golden threads: (1) a firm faith in a personal God who will lead us and protect us through all difficulties; (2) An unconditional love for other members which is immediately felt by those visiting the congregation; (3) Verbal efforts to encourage others to try these two life energizing experiences—faith and love. What if our goal setting process leaves out one or more of these principles?

One pastor led his people in a magnificently structured goaling program. They decided on the need for numerical growth. Methods were found and applied which involved calling on large numbers of non-members. The methods worked. The church began to grow. But while great energy was being expended in achieving growth, faith in God was displaced by faith in methods. Programs which helped people love one another were abandoned because all available energy was applied to reaching new people. As a result, the church grew for about a year, then leveled off. The group was somewhat larger now, but also more unhappy and irritable with each other. Concentration on reaching a valuable goal had blinded them to other equally important matters. Their goal was good, but not comprehensive enough.

The Pastor's Personal Interest Mirage: A pastor is generally good at weaving at least one of the three golden threads. If it is in the spiritual realm, he will likely achieve success there. At the same time, he may neglect the "love acted out" thread because he has little personal inclination in that direction. Or, he may be terrific at helping people to love each other, but very short on getting the verbal message to people outside the congregation. On the other hand, he may be excellent at mobilizing his army to make evangelism calls, but terrible at leading them to love one another after he gets them on the roll book.

Several food groups are needed for a balanced diet and healthy body. We need protein from the meat group, calcium from the milk group, carbohydrates from the bread-cereal group, and vitamins from the vegetable-fruit group. An increased volume in one category can't compensate for a total lack of other groups. Eating three times as many potatoes will not compensate for no green vegetables.

Multiple factors are also essential for healthy growth of the body of Christ, the church. Potatoes alone may make the organism feel full (busy?), but they just won't keep it healthy and growing. These pages spotlight many successful church growth aids. And each is a support for one of the three components. But don't let any one of these vitamin methods distract you from seeing the broader truth: All three must live together in the same congregation at the same time if it grows consistently over a period of years. If they don't, God cannot give us growth, no matter how hard we wave our little magic wands.

84

14

OTHER ROADBLOCKS

Why don't pastors rush out to learn more about the methods used by growing churches? Not because they do not wish their church to grow. Most ministers do desire growth (though they seldom admit it verbally due to its embarrassing absence in their parish). But in addition to the multiple perceptual difficulties already mentioned there are still other roadblocks which keep churchmen from learning and applying successful growth methods.

The Pendulum Syndrome Block: A pharmacist in Midwest City, Oklahoma, put it this way, "I've come up with a new law concerning religion. I call it Wilson's First Law—it's a takeoff on Newton's Third. *For every action, there's an unequal and opposite overreaction.* Over here we see churches that are dying from no emotion, no feeling, no caring about each other. So we say, 'That's completely wrong. Let's do something about it.'

"But on the opposite end of the pendulum is an emotionalism which has people speaking in tongues. I see glossolalia as a spin-off from a situation where the church isn't meeting people's needs. We certainly need to know that other people care for us. And we need to know that there is something more powerful than we are, something that will take care of us. And we need to know that this power can affect our daily life. But since the cold intellectualism in a lot of churches blocks that feeling, we now have an extreme overreaction in the opposite direction."

Nothing new about the Pendulum Syndrome. It has been going all through history, probably always will. But people in churches are often so preoccupied with whatever end of the pendulum they happen to be riding at the moment (or are opposed to) that their hot arguments obscure the need to work at evangelism regardless of what theological view they espouse.

The Mission-Nurture Dichotomy Block: Nurture means loving people and helping them to mature in Christ. Mission means doing the work of Christ in the world. Nurture is usually something done for people inside the church. Mission is what people inside the church do for people outside the church. Neither outranks the other, ever. There are times in history when one seems more needed than the other, but this is usually an illusion of the times. Both are eternally needed in equal dosage. Standing alone, each is a distortion of the total Word.

Jesus did both mission and nurture. He loved and taught the Twelve. But he also led them toward a point when they could go out and nurture others, which is mission. "A new commandment I give to you, that you love one another; even as I have loved you, that you also love one another." (John 13:34) That is nurture. But he also said, " . . . If any man would come after me, let him deny himself and take up his cross daily and follow me." (Luke 9:23) That is mission.

Adoption of either extreme, mission or nurture, as a singular pursuit can easily kill any congregation. It can even destroy a whole denomination. If we don't nurture people, the church will die from lack of numbers. People will not come to worship God in a place where they are not respected and loved. But if we don't offer people mission opportunities, the congregation will die from lack of quality. People will not continue participation in groups whose mission is too shallow. They are too busy for that. And they can easily find other clubs in the community which are visibly accomplishing something.

The Anti-Manipulation Block: Many churchpersons have an enormous abhorence of using gimics and insurance salesmen methods in winning people to Christ. A sensible fear. But this virtue can easily influence them to shrink back from *all* methods. Like the cat Mark Twain described who sat on a hot stove and would henceforth never get near any kind of stove, they have been burned by *one* method and now refuse to look at *any.*

Evangelistic growth is always a present potential anywhere. Even where population is not increasing, churches can grow. Statistics from numerous congregations which *are growing* validate Jesus' theory, "Do you not say, 'There are yet four months, then comes the harvest'? I tell you, lift up your eyes, and see how the fields are already white for harvest." (John 4:35)

But not unless the principles of harvesting are applied. A farmer does not expect results if he goes to the field with a plow instead of a combine. Nor does anything occur if he stays home altogether. Methods can certainly be overly relied on. Some have made little paper gods of their techniques. But most mainline denominations tend to the opposite extreme, using poor methods, wrong techniques, or no methods at all.

The Denominational Block: "That's too conservative (or too liberal). Our church just wouldn't go for something like that."

But specific techniques can often be kidnapped out of their sectarian context. It isn't always necessary to bring along the theological perspectives in which they are embedded. A delectable red apple sometimes hangs on a tree of fruit mostly consumed by worms. This does not mean you need to pick a whole bushel of bad apples. Nor does it mean you must cut down the whole tree in order to make apple dumplings.

The Analysis Paralysis Block: "Many of our young preachers are excellent at analysis, but weak on synthesis," observed an astute retired minister. "They can look over the whole arsenal of evangelism methods and point out the theological flaws in each one. But they seem incapable of pulling together truth from various sources and synthesizing it for a particular problem. Analysis is an interesting pastime, but good leadership requires synthesis."

It is not sufficient to become a mental microscope. Jesus did not tell us to go into all the world and figure out what is wrong with Samaritan theology, Greek worship rituals, or Jewish proselytizing. Such an approach would be like the man who went with a group of friends to a fine restaurant. He was so particular about food that he carefully inspected each new course. After making some critical remarks about each dish, he sent them back to the kitchen. The waitress was given careful instructions about what the cook should do to improve them. The whole evening passed with a great deal of informative conversation about food, but the man never ate any of it. As the group was leaving he was heard to say, "I really wasn't hungry anyway."

Some of these analyzation cop-outs come from the highly academic approach to ministerial education found in most seminaries. But more of it comes from our tendency to "reasonalize" (intelligent people reasonalize; stupid people rationalize) our own failure. It is so much easier to analyze the flaws in another man's theology than to work at the demanding task of synthesis.

One pastor took a group of his church leaders to visit a nearby Pentecostal church. He abhorred their theology, and was not about to adopt any of it. But that congregation had been growing rapidly during the past few years. His church had been quietly declining. So he hoped to learn whether any of their growth principles might be utilized in his own program. Such efforts to learn something from the opposition seem far more scientific (and Christian) than simply condemning their success as theologically unsound. The observation of other people is still one of God's greatest revelational instruments.

The Jerusalem church sent out an investigator, Barnabas, to check into the successful (but questionable) evangelism methods going on in Antioch. (Acts 11:20-22) From such observers, and the resulting Jerusalem Conference on Evangelism (Acts 15:1-29), they changed their membership policies. How fortunate for us American Christians that first century Jews were not too proud to learn from other congregations. Otherwise, we gentiles wouldn't even be in the church.

The Hard Work Block: Reasonalization is sometimes a veneer for something far more common—laziness. Many who claim theological hangups about particular methods actually have reservations more muscular than mental. Synthesis requires hard work. But the implementation of what is learned by synthesis may require even harder work.

The pastor of one growing church says, "One of the reasons we don't care for the spiritual needs of others is because it's such hard work. It means that every Monday night I stand there on a strange doorstep. The weather may be below freezing or snowing. And I'm there knocking on that door, scared to death, wondering what's going to be on the other side. That's hard work.

"It's an awful lot easier to get a basket of groceries together and take it out to somebody. They'll be glad to get it. Or, get together a hundred dollars and take it out to somebody who is poor. Or work to get somebody a job. They usually appreciate it. That kind of caring gets a positive response from people. But people do not feel their spiritual needs so keenly as they feel physical needs. That's why trying to meet these needs is often much harder work. But dare we forget that? Can we care about a man's calories and not care about his faith?"

The Inactive Member Block: "But we have so many members who don't come to church at all. Shouldn't we try to do something about them before we worry about total strangers?"

Such confusion clogs our arteries by encouraging us to concentrate on ourselves. That is not what evangelism is all about. We do need to activate inactives. Much thought and energy should be sent this direction. But churches don't enlarge by adding members who already belong. Growth comes by attracting people from outside our fellowship.

A pastor puts it this way, "I don't care what the method of evangelism is, or how hard you work at it; a certain number will become inactive. Look at any other organization, Rotary Club for instance. Even with their terrific stress on attendance, members become inactive. Even if a person pays a thousand dollars to take a course, a certain number will become irresponsible dropouts. There is no way you can keep some people from being irresponsible. It's imperative to agonize over that, but you can't let that keep you from trying to win five others. Unless you are constantly finding new people, this church or any church, is going to die. The idea that we ought to forget about quantity and work on quality is just not realistic."

The Numbers Game Block: "I don't want to get involved in playing the numbers game. We should be concerned about people, not numbers," said one young minister.

Right. But that's only one end of another great paradox whose opposite is also true. "If you don't pay attention to numbers, you soon won't need to pay attention to anything else," says the business manager in a regional headquarters. "Soon there won't be anything left to pay attention to."

The young pastor was irritated by the way he had heard two preachers talking following a revival. They sounded like Indian war chiefs counting scalps after a raiding party. That's tragic. But numbers are also symbols for people—people for whom Christ died and people in whom Christ is interested. Those kind of numbers are something sacred.

Most congregations and denominations keep good records of stewardship and mission giving. We aren't scared of numbers when we talk about money. On the contrary, we often take pride in figures which represent dollars. Why the inconsistency of attitude about numbers? Could it be because we are less successful in body growth, so the numbers don't lift our ego much? Or could it be that worrying about dollar numbers is not such hard work as worrying about people numbers?

With all these natural hindrances, how can a pastor possibly keep his balance in trying to pass the *word*? With great difficulty. The pressure to ride off into the sunset on a personal hobby horse is greater than most can withstand. But if the pastor doesn't find the balance, nobody in the church is likely to lead a charge in that direction. So how can a person put a level to his ministry and find out whether it is out of balance?

One way is to title three sheets of paper with *Being the Word, Doing the Word, Saying the Word.* Then list the various activities of the church under these headings. Looking at your appointment book and church calendar for last year will help your memory here. After this, take several days to brainstorm with yourself about programs that might start you toward some corrective action. Better still, do the same thing with your evangelism committee, your church board, or several groups in the church. This adds to thoroughness while increasing the appreciation of members for the value of their church programs. Making a list often tells us that more is already happening than we thought. If it should do the opposite, we need to have the courage to face that.

In this process, the pastor must ask himself some hard questions: Am I encouraging people to set goals for prayer and Bible study in the same way that I help them set mission giving goals? Am I working as hard to set numerical growth goals as I am at meeting world hunger needs? Am I leading people in helping meet community needs with the same fervency that I use in looking for church school teachers? Do I work as hard in calling on worship visitors as I do in urging people to attend a church convention? Am I setting goals for church growth with the same drive I use in seeking appropriate figures for the annual budget? Do I work as hard at organizing evangelistic calling as I do to get people to raise their stewardship levels?

Such questions are hard to answer. Self-perception about *word* balance is deathly difficult. Socrates said, "Know thyself." That is easier to voice than to accomplish, especially here.

After these tough questions are faced, what next? After a pastor has diagnosed a case of laryngitis *saying* or paralyzed *doing* or anemic *being,* what next? How to correct the malady? Just as there is no simple prescription for finding the sick spots, there is no universal penicillin for correcting them.

A number of excellent balancing measures are illustrated in these chapters. But finding the specific subtechnique needed in a particular congregation is much more complex than a written band-aid. Methods must be appropriate to the history and personality of each church. The type of people trying to be reached in the community must also be considered. This requires time and energy, testing different possibilities, experimenting until the right antibiotic is found for the ill system. But then, that's why people see a physician instead of doing it themselves; because they want perceptive leadership. And that's why churches hire professional leaders, isn't it? To do just that, give leadership.

Part VI

Getting Started

15

FROM THE INSIDE OUT

The hobby of a Methodist bishop in the early part of this century was sharpshooting. One of the bishop's friends, while visiting his farm one day, went for a stroll. Walking down a lane he noticed on several fenceposts a crudely painted little bull's-eye. Looking closer, he saw that exactly in the middle of each target was a bullet hole. "The bishop must be a remarkable rifleman," he thought. "He hits everything he shoots at." As the two men were having dinner that evening, he mentioned the fenceposts, complimenting the bishop on his marksmanship.

"Oh, that," the bishop replied with a twinkle in his eyes. "Those are easy to explain. You see, I shot at the post and then drew a circle around the bullet hole."

This unfortunately describes the attitude of many churches after they become financially secure and well established. Instead of continuing to set new goals, they start accepting whatever they happen to hit by accident.

We have all heard of business and professional men who write daily, monthly, and yearly goals on calendars or in their date books. Then they check off items on their "do-it" agendas as particular objectives are reached.

The lives of most great men tell the same story. Their greatness did not come about by sheer accident. They often held clear-cut goals firmly in mind for a long period of time. This principle also applies to churches. The reason many congregations don't grow is because they have never decided to. They are engaged in a comfortable drifting process that carries them everywhere in general but no place in particular.

Churches that grew, without exception, did so because they intended to. A congregation which grew from 315 to 821 in five years set a goal of one thousand members to be reached by January 1, 1976. While the goal was not quite attained, it certainly shaped the direction of efforts. They began by having members write down in some detail their dreams and aspirations for the life of the church. This was done in a series of six dinners in which more than three hundred participated. Task force committees then took these ideas and solidified them into concise phrases. Those goals then went to the official board; from the official board to the congregation. That was in 1970. Some of the goals were reached; some were not. Some have been exceeded. The pastor concludes, "If you don't know where you're going or what you are going to do, you are not likely to do very much."

Good methods for congregational goal setting are available in printed guides from many sources. In evangelism, one method might be to review the three golden threads at a fellowship dinner involving the entire congregation. Then the group could be broken up so that each table brainstorms for ideas of how each of the threads might be strengthened in their church. Another method would be to break up by departments, committees, church school classes, and study groups.

A successful businessman says, "Dreams are the stuff that success is made of. But you must first *have a dream* before it can come true." And that is the point at which many churches need to start. They don't really have a dream. So somebody must help them to get one.

Care should be taken to assure people that we are not just trying to make our church bigger. We are seeking to fulfill the primary purposes for which the church was established to begin with: (1) to love God; (2) love neighbor; (3) to spread the word about these two ideas to others. In short, we are attempting by such brainstorming and goal setting to be faithful to the gospel.

The emphasis should be placed on dreaming about the future; while refusing to discuss what such goals might cost in dollars. The stress should be on thinking about what God may want us to do.

The mechanics of how to do it should be left for later. If we dream according to God's purposes for us, he will usually help us find methods for their accomplishment. But that may take much more time than is required to find the dream itself.

It may be useful to introduce the seven universal roadblocks to congregational progress: (1) We've never done it that way; (2) We're not ready for that; (3) We're doing all right without it; (4) We tried that once before; (5) It costs too much; (6) That's not our responsibility; (7) It just won't work. Anyone who voices one of these phrases at a goal setting meeting should be good-naturedly fined a quarter. The quarters should then be used to buy a book for the church library on the subject of optimism.

The biggest untapped resource in any church is the imagination of its members. Have meetings of key leaders for the express purpose of dreaming dreams. Think big. Use your imagination to visualize the kind of congregation you wish to become. Never let anyone make fun of the dreaming process. It was a dreamer who discovered America. It was a dreamer who discovered the first anesthetic; found the Salk vaccine for polio; brought about the first prison reform in England. It was a dreamer named Livingston who pioneered the work of Christianity on the continent of Africa. It is not the dreamers who waste our time in churches. It is the cold realists who are trapped in the dead shell of what they can see and feel this very moment.

Down in the little town of Diamond, Missouri, in the year of 1864 a black boy was born. Almost from the beginning, this boy was different. He dreamed that even a black child could amount to something. When he got bigger he had another dream. He thought that even the common worthless peanut could amount to something if someone gave it half a chance. He did, and it did: George Washington Carver.

In North Carolina during the year of 1903, two brothers had some crazy dreams about flying. They actually thought a machine could be constructed that would allow people to sail through the air like they sailed on water—perhaps even carry cargo that way. Orville and Wilbur Wright, and the dream flew.

In 1215 a group of English noblemen forced King John to sign a piece of paper called the Magna Carta. Why? They were men with dreams about a free society. And the dreams flew. That paper eventually blossomed into our present legal system.

In the late 1800s thousands of immigrants put their feet down on Ellis Island in New York harbor. They looked up at a statue which said, "I lift my lamp beside the golden door." They came from poor farms in Ireland. Pushed out by poverty, yes. But more than that, pushed out by their dreams. The Mayflower was the same thing—a boatload of dreamers—people with no freedom of religion in their history. But they didn't need it there. They had it in their heads and hearts. And the dream flew.

In the mid-ninteenth century, Harriet Beecher Stowe began to dream that black people ought not to be slaves. She put that dream into the words of a book—*Uncle Tom's Cabin*. And the dream flew.

The Bible repeats that story again and again—Abraham dreaming of a promised land he had never seen. Paul, sitting in Antioch with a dream about preaching the gospel to all the gentiles in the whole world. A bunch of itinerant disciples driven across the decaying Roman empire by the fresh-born dream of a world for Christ. And the dream flew.

In the movie "Paint Your Wagon," Lee Marvin plays a philosophical drunk named Ben Rumstead. During the closing scene, Ben Rumstead is standing in the rain of a muddy street talking with the proprietor of a local store. The store owner looks at the passing wagons, loaded with people and furniture moving out of town, and says, "There are two kinds of people in this world. There are those who move on and those that stay. Ain't that the truth, Ben Rumstead?"

"No, that ain't the truth," Ben Rumstead replies, with a swagger enlarged by the half-empty bottle in his hand. "There are two kinds of people in this world. Them that is going someplace and them that is going noplace. *That's* the truth."

Ben Rumstead's principle applies equally well to congregations. And those who are going someplace always have a dream in their head. So if yours doesn't have one, get one. And if you've got one, hang onto it.

16

FROM THE OUTSIDE IN

The receptionist picks up the phone on the first ring. A young pastor from the southern part of the state wants to speak with the staff person in charge of evangelism. They are connected and exchange the customary irrelevancies.

"I have a problem I thought you might be able to give me some advice on," the pastor says. "A lot of new people are moving into our area. The town is growing. But our church isn't. I just frankly don't know where to begin. They really didn't cover this in seminary. Is there some kind of plan or program you could suggest?"

The staff person is sympathetic. After several minutes of listening, he says, "It sure is frustrating to know something ought to be happening, yet not be able to get it done. But evangelism is really hard everywhere these days. People are involved in so many other things besides church. Say, I understand that the Bradberry Church is going to be open next month. You might want to be considered for that. You have been where you are for three years. I thought maybe. . . ."

Various models of such conversations occur with astonishing frequency. One young minister contacted denominational people in his district, then his conference, then the national office. No one he talked with could suggest any concrete plan for assisting a congregation in evangelism. Had he wanted to build a new building, a consulting team would have arrived the following week. They would have plans, manuals, all kinds of options and expertise. Had he wanted to conduct a missions workshop, three resource leaders and two programs could have been listed instantly. Had he asked for help in raising money, an excellent plan would have been in the afternoon mail. In Christian education, someone was available to do a teacher training workshop, recommend curriculum resources, etc., ad infinitum. But since the problem was people rather than bricks or dollars, nobody knew what to say.

A new phobia has frozen denominational leaders into silence for the last twenty years. "Evangelism program phobia" will not be found in the standard psychiatric handbook. But the fear of recommending concrete evangelism methods is a common emotional illness in ecclesiastical personalities. Leaders made a unanimous response to bad programs and good programs poorly done. They advocated that all programs be scrapped. This logic is equivalent to dropping construction on a church because several members complain about the size of the ladies' restroom.

It is unlikely that any perfect church growth program will be developed to fit every congregation. That would be like recommending a universal blueprint from which all new church buildings would be erected. But floundering congregations and inexperienced pastors need some ideas about where to start. The remainder of this chapter is not meant to be a universal plan. It is an attempt to illustrate what might be done from the outside in when a congregation yells for help.

"I'm going to send you a three page information sheet which I'd like your church board or evangelism department to fill out. This will help me get a good picture of your congregation's personality. We need to set up a date when I can have three sessions with your entire congregation—as many people as you can possibly get to attend. It is important that we work with all your people; not just the select few who agreed to be on the evangelism committee this year.

"What we need is either a weekend or three evenings during the week—whatever would be most convenient for your people. In the first session, we will do some inspirational work to get people thinking in terms of possibilities instead of negatives. During that time we will also review their growth history and current situation, using the material they have already prepared. We will complete that first session by reviewing the principles which produce growth in a congregation. Just as there are known principles by which money is raised or building programs undertaken, certain universals also underly congregational growth. If these principles are applied, growth generally results. If part of them are used, less growth happens. If none are used, decline has probably set in. Your people need to understand what these principles are. After that, they can begin to focus on how they might be applied to their situation.

"At the second session, we will work at setting growth goals for your church. Some of this will be done by splitting up into the various classes and interest groups which already exist in your church. These groups will buzz together and set the goals for their specific group. In other words, once we know what the growth principles are, then we can decide what goals we want to set in light of these principles.

"At the third session, we will spend time selecting the exact methods which the church might use to achieve the goals they have set the previous evening. In other words, the goals are set by your people in light of the universal growth principles. Then, methods are discussed which might be helpful in trying to achieve these goals. The methods suggested will vary according to your local situation and the inclination of your people.

"During that last session, we will also set the date for a check-up meeting about three months from then. At that time, I will return to discuss how the methods are working. In the light of their experiences, some methods may need to be changed. Some may have to be discarded as unworkable in your community. Others may need to be added. The check-up meeting is important because: (1) It gives your people a definite target date toward which they can work; (2) It provides an opportunity for objective evaluation from the outside; (3) It gives a chance for mid-course corrections as an alternative to dropping the whole program because some part of it isn't working; (4) It gives you, as pastor, some outside person who can serve as a catalyst in ways that you cannot; (5) If some part of the method fails, you will not take the blame for it personally."

Advance Preparation

ANALYZING YOUR CONGREGATION'S PERSONALITY

Note: This sample form is to be filled out by the entire church board at meetings held prior to the Church Growth Seminar itself. All blanks must be completed, as the information requested is very important in conducting a successful seminar experience.

1. Indicate the numbers of your present members related to these vocations:

_____Business

_____Clerical

_____College Students

_____Executives

_____Farmers and Ranchers

_____Laborers

_____Professionals like physicians, dentists, teachers

_____Retired Persons

_____Grade School and High School Students

_____Housewives

2. Indicate the numbers of your present active members who fall into these age groups:

_____under 10

_____10 to 20

_____20 to 40

_____40 to 60

_____over 60

3. How many interest groups and classes exist in your church? They might include some of the following examples, but might also include several others. Be thorough in your listing. Where a group has several subgroups, list these also.

_____Men's Organization

_____Women's Organization

_____Adult Choir

_____Children's Choir

_____Jr. High Evening Youth Group

_____Sr. High Evening Youth Group

_____Adult Prayer Group

_____Adult Weekday Study Group

_____College Fellowship Group

_____Singles Group

_____Church School Classes

Others: _____

_____

_____

_____

4. What is your total participating church membership at present?
5. Divide the total participating membership by the number of groups listed above. This figure equals _____.
6. What percentage of meeting time do your church board, departments, and committees devote to discussing and planning for church growth? Make an estimate.

7. How many face-to-face contacts do laypersons make each week with non-members for the purpose of trying to influence them toward the church? _____

8. How many face-to-face contacts does the pastor(s) make each week with non-members for the purpose of trying to influence them toward the church? _____

9. How many "maintenance workers" do you have in the church? _____ A "maintenance worker" is any person who gives time and energy to helping with the programs which the church runs for those presently attending.

10. How many "church growth workers" do you have in the church? _____ A "church growth worker" is one who does face-to-face work in trying to reach the unchurched each week.

11. What methods do you presently use to reach out to prospective members in a warm, friendly, accepting manner?

12. What methods do you use to put prospective members into social contact with present church members in a one-to-one and small group basis?

13. Of the last ten adults who joined your church, how many months passed before each was asked to assume a responsibility in the church?

14. Indicate the number of persons who have joined your church in the last three years?

_____under 20

_____20 to 40

_____40 to 60

_____over 60

15. What methods are presently being used by your church school teachers to increase the growth rate of their classes?

16. When was the last time your church systematically evaluated its growth pattern?

17. When was the congregation's last evangelism training event?

18. When was the last time your congregation set specific numerical goals for church growth?

19. What system do you presently use to find the names and addresss of persons who might be prospective members of your church?

20. Of all the present programs and activities sponsored by your church at the present time, which in your opinion are your greatest strengths? In other words, what programs and activities are you the proudest of at the present time?

The following will be prepared by the seminar leader's office and presented at the first session:

21. Chart on graph paper the growth pattern of your church membership and church school enrollment for the last fifteen years. This is available through most denominational yearbooks.

22. What is the population growth pattern of your community? United States Census Reports are available in your local library. More current statistics are available in "Sales Management Magazine," which may be obtained from your local Chamber of Commerce.
23. How would you describe the age distribution of people who live in your community?

First Session, or Evening, of the Seminar

Begin with a good mind stretcher, like the film "How to Grow a Church,"[1] This helps people catch the vision that churches can grow and are growing in many places.

Following the film, the seminar leader may want to introduce the growth principles with something like the following: The first thing I want to talk about is confusion. There is confusion in most churches about a lot of things, but especially about evangelism. A family was vacationing in the Blue Ridge Mountains in eastern Tennessee. Since the little boy in the family had just obtained a pet squirrel, he refused to be parted from the little animal. So Dad stoically loaded squirrel and cage into the front luggage compartment of their small foreign car. Stopping at a crossroads filling station back up in the mountains, an old man with a white beard came out. While he was gassing up the car, the family walked over to a nearby lookout point to enjoy the view. Coming back, the father asked, "What do I owe you?"

"Don't rightly know," the old man replied.

"What do you mean, you don't know?" the father said.

"Well, I gave your engine some peanuts, but I'll be darned if I know how to check its oil."

Evangelism is much the same. There is much confusion about what makes it go. There is no confusion about knowing that we *ought* to do it. Jesus said, "Go into all the world and make disciples." (paraphrase of Matthew 28:19) We know that. We have heard it all our lives. And there is no confusion about wanting to do it. Most of us do want our church to grow. But there is much confusion about *how* to do it.

An easterner who had never seen a real live horse came west to vacation on a dude ranch. Early in the morning one of the hands encountered him out by the barn, trying to saddle a horse. But he was putting the saddle on backwards. Trying to be politely diplomatic, the weathered wrangler inquired, "Say, did you know you were putting that saddle on backwards?"

"What do you mean?" the tenderfoot replied indigently. "You don't even know which way I'm going."

It doesn't matter how enthusiastic you are about going someplace. If you don't know how, you are in trouble. You may get there by accident. On the other hand, you may not.

At this point, the seminar leader may want to tell a real life story of some church which has recently achieved great growth. If he has had personal experience in a growing church, he will want to use that as an illustration.

Following the illustrations, he could say something like the following: "Through a study of this church and other growing churches across the country, we have begun to isolate the principles that produce church growth anyplace, anytime. We will now take a look at some of these."

An overhead projector is a helpful tool for this phase. Thus, each principle can be seen in isolation from the others. As each is thrown on the screen, the leader may wish to make an illustrative comment about it.

1. The laypersons in a growing church believe that a church which is faithful to the gospel is seeking to grow and that winning new people to Christ is among their most important tasks.

2. The pastor(s) in a growing church keep in constant touch with the present growth statistics, constantly trys new ways of improving skills at this work, gives a large amount of time to promoting church growth, and leads laypersons in this work by showing them how as well as by telling them how.

3. The members of a growing church have positive attitudes toward their church.

4. Large numbers of members in a growing church are praying for the guidance of God's Holy Spirit and for specific non-members by name.

5. Members of a growing church constantly reach out to new people in a warm, friendly, accepting manner, promoting opportunities for frequent, one-to-one and small group contacts of new people with present members.

6. A growing church has a growing church school attendance.

7. The church school teachers of a growing church see the work of growth as an important part of their teaching responsibility.

8. A growing church has a large number of regularly meeting small groups or classes designed to meet a large variety of interests.

9. A growing church finds that much of its growth comes from winning people of similar age, occupational, educational, and financial levels to presently existing interest groups or classes.

10. A growing church frequently forms totally new interest groups or classes by drawing together persons of similar age, occupational, educational, and financial levels.

11. A growing church quickly involves all new members in some responsibility in the church.

12. A growing church quickly involves all new members in at least one class or interest group within the church.

13. Members of a growing church make a large number of face-to-face contacts each week with non-members who they are trying to influence toward the church.

14. The pastor(s) of a growing church makes a large number of face-to-face contacts each week with non-members who they are trying to influence toward the church.

15. A growing church has a systematic method for obtaining large numbers of names and addresses of non-church members, especially relatives, friends, and acquaintances of present members.

16. A growing church strives to make its number of "church growth workers" equal to its number of "maintenance workers." A church growth worker is one who does face-to-face work in trying to influence the unchurched. A maintenance worker is one who works in the program which the church runs for those presently attending.

17. The board, departments, and committees of a growing church spend a large percentage of their meeting time discussing and planning for church growth.

18. A growing church constantly charts its membership and church school attendance and displays these prominently in the room where board, department, and committee meetings usually take place.

19. A growing church sets specific times for church growth progress evaluations, at which time all methods are evaluated and modified through discussing the experiences of the past few months.

20. A growing church involves the total membership of the church in setting goals for growth.

21. A growing church has regular church growth training sessions for the entire membership.

Following the presentation of these principles, it is helpful to review the present congregational personality pattern—the one prepared on a three page form prior to his arrival. It is helpful to have this reproduced for the overhead projector. There is no direct comparison with the afore mentioned principles, but these will begin to form in people's minds.

Along with the congregational personality overview, the leader may want to add perspective by highlighting the city or county population changes in a manner like the following:

1920	1,473
1930	2,314
1940	2,026
1950	1,443
1960	1,605
1970	3,657

He may also wish to prepare a sheet which shows the membership trend in that congregation as compared with membership trends in other congregations of that denomination in the same part of the state.

The following is one line from how such a sheet might look. It is taken from a chart showing the same figures for thirty-seven other churches:

Church & County	1961	1971	1975	% Change	1960-70 Cnty. Pop. Change
Bennett-Proctor County	190	155	135	−25.9%	+14.7%

A membership and church school graph for the last fifteen years makes another good visualization.

Active Church Membership and Church School Attendance

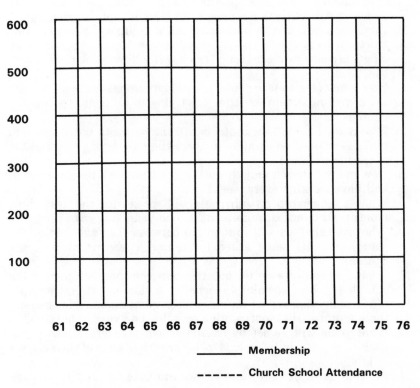

_____ Membership

_ _ _ _ _ _ Church School Attendance

103

Second Session, or Evening, of the Seminar

By this time, the congregation has begun to see the gap between what they are doing and what they ought to be doing. Along with that, they have begun to understand that methods are available by which they might change their pattern.

They are now ready to set goals for themselves. Part of this can be done with the entire group together. Sunday school classes and other groups should be given a chance to caucus during the evening. They will set concrete goals and report back to the total congregation so that a composite picture of all goals may be seen by everyone. Answering the following seventeen questions will help people to set the kinds of goals which produce growth. Instead of centering on evangelism generalities, they help people focus on the specific growth factors.

1. Exactly what attitudes will we seek to promote in our church?
2. How many of our members will we seek to involve in prayer for growth?
3. How much time will we devote in each board, department and committee meeting to discussion and planning for church growth?
4. How many new people will each interest group or class seek to attract?
5. How may new interest groups or classes will we seek to establish this year?
6. How many face-to-face contacts will laypersons seek to make each week with non-members they are trying to influence toward the church?
7. How many face-to-face contacts will the pastor or pastors seek to make each week with non-members they are trying to influence toward the church?
8. How many "church growth workers" will we seek to enlist, train, and have working every week?
9. What membership growth goals will we set for the next three months, six months, nine months, one year, five years?
10. What goal shall we set (in months) between the adult joining the church and his being asked to assume a responsibility in the church.
11. What goal shall we set (in months) between the adult joining the church and his becoming involved in a class or interest group?
12. What goals shall we set for church school attendance in the next three months, six months, nine months, one year, five years?
13. What goals will be set by church school teachers, youth group leaders, and study group leaders for growth in each of their classes or groups?
14. At what meeting and date will we evaluate our growth pattern

every three months?

15. How frequently will we establish evangelism training events for our leaders and people?
16. How many of our congregation's members will we try to involve in setting our goals for church growth each year?
17. How many names and addresses of persons who might be interested in our church will we try to obtain each week?

Third Session, or Evening, of the Seminar

Here, time can be spent selecting and outlining the methods which various classes and groups might use to help achieve their goals. If feasible, the leader can meet with various groups during the day to give suggestions concerning methods they might wish to try. In moving on from goals to methods, the leader may begin by asking, "What methods shall we use in order to achieve the goals we set for ourselves last night? Dreams must have landing gears as well as wings. Otherwise, they can't take off. So how shall we get started?"

By this time, people will have an openness to the kinds of methods the leader may suggest. Had he started with the methods at the first session, they would likely have rejected most of them.

At this session, a *Church Growth Team* should be appointed to give continuing leadership to the congregation for the next months and year. This should never be the evangelism committee. Such an approach narrows the spectrum of involvement and leaves out many of the persons whose efforts are essential to growth. The team should include the following key leaders:

A Church Growth Superintendent
A Church Growth Statistician
A Leadership Development Superintendent
The Pastor
All Church School Teachers
Chairpersons from Elders, Deacons, and Deaconesses Groups
Youth Group Sponsors
Board Chairperson

The *Church Growth Superintendent* will be the general chairperson. The *Leadership Development Superintendent* will see that all new members become quickly involved and integrated into the life of the church. The most important task is probably that of *Church Statistician*. This person should be highly competent at record keeping and detail work. He or she will keep the congregation constantly informed about where they are and where they seem to be headed.

The seminar leader will give the *Church Statistician* instructions on how to prepare and keep up-to-date six charts. These charts will be constantly displayed on the walls of the room where the board, departments, and committees meet:

1. A chart of fifteen years of membership and church school enrollment or attendance. These figures can be obtained from denominational yearbook records.

2. A twelve month current year chart of membership, church attendance, and church school attendance.

3. A fifty-two week chart showing the number of contacts laypersons and pastor(s) are making with non-church members.

4. A fifty-two week chart showing the total number of church members making contacts with non-members each week.

5. A twelve month chart showing membership additions for the current year.

6. A chart showing the size of each present class and group, plus the growth goal each has set for itself. These would be "United Fund type" thermometers, with extensions showing the goals and the date achieved.

Chart 1

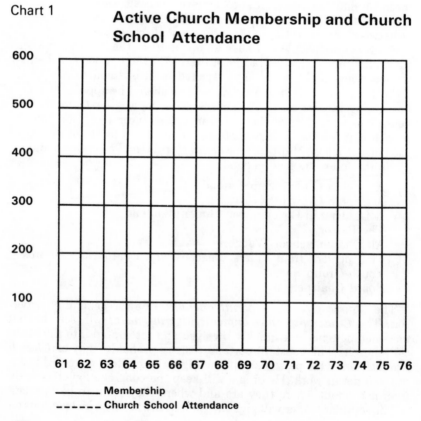

Active Church Membership and Church School Attendance

——————— Membership

– – – – – – Church School Attendance

Chart 2

Membership, Church Attendance and Sunday School Attendance

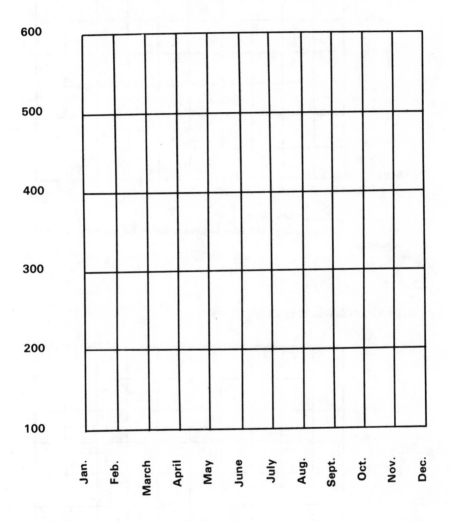

.... Morning Worship Attendance
._____ Church School Attendance
_____ Church Membership

Chart 3

Contacts with Prospective Members

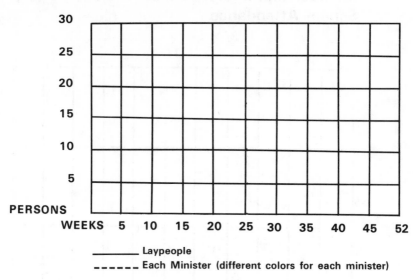

_____ Laypeople
_ _ _ _ _ Each Minister (different colors for each minister)

Chart 4

Total Church Growth Workers

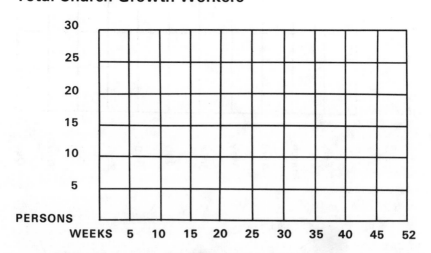

Each must make at least 1 call per week on a non-church member, or turn in the name of at least 1 prospective member per week.

108

Chart 5

Membership Additions for Current Year

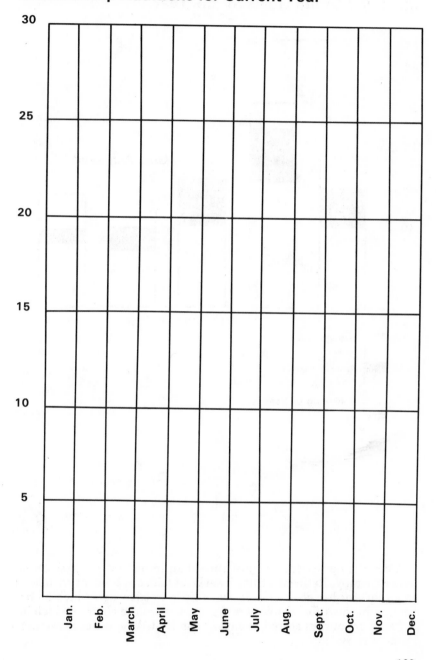

Chart 6

Class and Group Goals for the Year

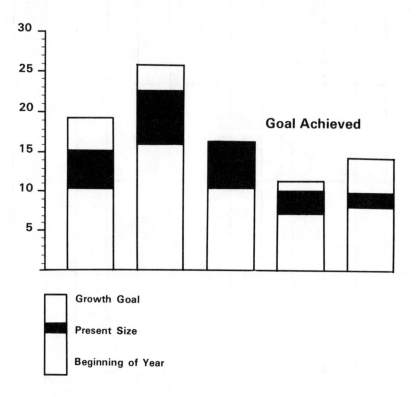

A counseling patient had just turned an important progress corner in her therapy. Returning from a weekend trip, she brought with her a small gift for her counselor. It was a little wooden sign which he has kept on his desk for many years. Facing toward the chair in which his patients are always seated, it says, "The Best Way to Get Something Done is to Begin."

BIBLIOGRAPHY

Chapter 1

1. All statistics on congregations taken from the 1970-71 and 1976 editions of *Year Book and Directory of the Christian Church (Disciples of Christ)* (Indianapolis, Indiana: The General Office of the Christian Church—Disciples of Christ).

2. All population figures for 1970 taken from *U.S. Census Population Reports.* All population figures for 1974 taken from *Sales Management,* November 1974.

3. Information and quotes taken from tape-recorded conversations with Ken Cole and members of his First Christian Church congregation in Ruidoso, New Mexico, during January 1976.

4. Information and quotes taken from a tape-recorded conversation with Herb Leslie, pastor of Sandy Springs Christian Church in Atlanta, Georgia, during February 1976.

5. Information and quotes taken from tape-recorded interviews with James C. Baughman and from mimeographed material entitled "Keeping Your Worms Warm," produced at Middletown Christian Church, Middletown, Kentucky, 1975.

6. This excellent system is described in a helpful booklet entitled "Keeping Your Worms Warm." It may be obtained by sending one dollar to Dr. James Baughman, Middletown Christian Church, Box 43266, Middletown, Kentucky 40243.

Chapter 3

1. Paul Tillich, *Dynamics of Faith.* Harper & Brothers, 1957, p. 8.

2. William Barclay, as quoted by J. D. Douglas, "William Barclay, Extraordinary Communicator," *Christianity Today,* January 16, 1976, p. 6.

3. First Christian Church Newsletter (mimeo), Keokuk, Iowa. January 1976.

Chapter 4

1. Paul Tournier, *The Meaning of Persons.* Harper & Row, 1973, p. 193.

2. *Ibid., Dynamics of Faith,* pp. 23-24.

Chapter 5

1. Samuel M. Shoemaker, *Receive Thy Church Beginning with Me.* Harper & Brothers, 1948, p. 24.

Chapter 6

1. Elton Trueblood, *The New Man for Our Time.* Harper & Row, 1970, p. 26.

2. Toyohiko Kagawa, *Love the Law of Life*. The John C. Winston Company, 1929, p. 286.

3. Dietrich Bonhoeffer, *The Cost of Discipleship*. The Macmillan Company, 1959, p. 174.

Chapter 7

1. Question and answer column, "Can We Help You?" *Church Management: The Clergy Journal,* February 1975.

Chapter 8

1. Dudley Strain, *The Measure of a Minister*. The Bethany Press, 1964, p. 13.

2. T. R. Glover, *Quote* February 22, 1976.

3. Bonhoeffer, *The Cost of Discipleship,* p. 30.

4. Rollo Walter Brown, "An Observer Warns the Church," *Harper's Magazine,* December 1937, p. 18, 19.

Chapter 11

1. Lillian Eichler Watson, ed., *Light from Many Lamps*. Simon and Schuster, 1951, p. 67.

2. E. Stanley Jones, *A Song of Ascents*. New Abingdon, 1968, p. 361.

Chapter 13

1. Robert Raines, *Reshaping the Christian Life*. Harper & Row, 1964, p. 67.

Chapter 16

1. May be obtained from Christian Communication, 1857 Highland Oaks Drive, Arcadia, California 91006.

Discussion Ideas
for Adult Groups Using
EVANGELISM'S OPEN SECRETS

Instructions for Leaders:
This material is suitable for seven or more sessions of group study. It may be used in adult classes, retreats, evangelism committees, or other discussion groups. Evangelism committees will find the discussion questions a particularly helpful tool. From this base, a group can move from evaluation of the local program toward recognition of what directions need to be pursued in making evangelistic growth a reality instead of a vague dream.

SESSION 1. Introduction: Framing the Picture (pages 7-10)
1. What is the actual record of growth or decline of our congregation over the past ten years? What is your evaluation of this record?
2. How have our membership statistics been determined and reported to the annual statistical report of our denomination?
3. How does our denomination define the differences between participating and non-participating members? Our congregation? Discuss.
4. What is the population growth pattern of our surrounding community during the past ten years?
5. How do you assess the *growth potential* and the *will to grow* of this congregation?
6. To what degree do we agree or disagree with the definition "Evangelism is defined herein as the winning of the allegiance of new persons to the Lordship of Jesus Christ"? (page 9)

Resources:
A. 10-year membership report
B. The annual statistical report of your denomination
C. Definition of participating and non-participating member found in the annual statistical report of our denomination
D. Chamber of Commerce or U.S. Census community population figures for the last ten years

SESSION 2. Part I—Demythologizing Church Growth (pages 11-23)
1. Three Golden Threads (chapter 1, pages 11-18)
   A. List and discuss what you think our congregation (ministers and laypersons) should do in order to grow numerically.
   B. Can you give illustrations of the "oversimplificationitis" disease to which Miller refers on the top of page 12?
   C. List and discuss what our congregation is doing and/or could do better under the three golden threads of "Being

the Word, Doing the Word, and Saying the Word." Where are we strongest and weakest?
  2. Today's Invisible Heresies (chapter 2, pages 19-23)
     A. Study and discuss the following passages
        Romans 10:14—"Saying the Word"
        James 2:17—"Doing the Word"
        John 15:14—"Being the Word"
     What are our church's invisible heresies?

SESSION 3. Part II—Saying the Word (pages 24-43)
  1. Contact Cement (chapter 3, pages 24-31)
     A. Discuss ways to contact people outside the church. Discuss ways to recruit callers and grouping of callers. Describe "decision calls." Why is it important to make calls on each "not-yet-member"?
     B. List the reasons why you think these are helpful methods: Egg Roll Evangelism, Mother's Day Out, and publicity.
     C. Give examples of these reasons for contact failure from your personal experience: Importance of the personal touch; verbalization concern; and repetition.
     D. List all the ideas you can think of which our church should use in maintaining contact with "not yet members."

  2. Good News by Modern Persons (chapter 4, pages 32-37)
     A. Illustrate from your own experience the difference between objective witnessing and objectionable witnessing.
     B. Personality presence: Give examples of "Good News by Modern Persons."
     C. Why is verbal communication so important?
     D. Discuss nonverbal communication.
  3. Saints Under Construction (chapter 5, pages 38-43)
     A. It is possible to affirm people without affirming their poor behavior? How? Do you know any individuals who seem to do this well?
     B. List ways in which we should be sensitive to the needs of new or visiting families.
     C. Name some roadblocks used frequently by our church members.
     D. What does it mean to be an accepting church?

SESSION 4. Part III—Doing the Word (pages 44-61)
  1. Love Is an Inside Job (chapter 6, pages 44-48)
     A. Do our church members show real concern and love for one another? Do we show equal love for those outside the church?
     B. Name some needs of persons within the church.
     C. Name some needs of persons outside the church.

D. In what ways are we guilty of trying to express love *without taking action?*
2. Gathering Two or Three (chapter 7, pages 49-54)
   A. What one thing does Miller say everyone is looking for in church membership?
   B. Name all the different types of group structures you can think of in our congregation.
   C. Talk about our youth programs and how they relate to our evangelism work.
   D. What are some suggestions for starting new adult groups?
3. God's Quarterback (chapter 8, pages 55-61)
   A. What qualities should the leader of a growing congregation possess?
   B. What about his convictions?
   C. Preaching?
   D. Administrative leadership?

SESSION 5. Part IV—*Being the Word (pages 62-76)*
1. First Rung on Any Ladder (chapter 9, pages 62-66)
   A. Discuss Miller's statement: "Without the faith that God wants evangelism done, and without the faith that he will help us do it, little happens." (page 62)
   B. Describe the faith exercised by Abrahams, Moses, and Isaiah. Read together Hebrews 11.
   C. The central question is *faith in whom?* Ourselves? God? Or both?
   D. Name some persons you personally know who have seemingly been untouched by God's love.
2. Sold on the Product (chapter 10, pages 67-70)
   A. Discuss what God has done in your life to cause you to be "sold on the product."
   B. Miller suggests three questions as a first step toward evangelism in many congregations (page 70). Discuss these.
3. Hitch Your Wagon to the Spirit (chapter 11, pages 71-76)
   A. If your class named earlier in this lesson any persons who have not yet been reached by God's love, pray for them by name right now!
   B. What would happen if we prayed for such a list of persons every week in our class?

SESSION 6. Part V—*Overcoming Theological Hangups (pages 77-90)*
1. God or Methods? (chapter 12, 77-79)
   A. Can you give personal illustrations of the truth in the following two statements?
      (1) "Evangelism is not something we do; it is something God does through us." (page 77)
      (2) "Pray as if it all depends on God. Work as if it all depends on you." (page 77)

B. List all the ways you can think of in which God's Word comes to a person.

2. Mirages Get in Our Eyes (chapter 13, pages 80-84)
   A. Be sure you understand these past and present mirages. See if individuals can give at least one concrete illustration or each mirage from their own experience:
      (1) Pietism—religious self-righteousness (page 81)
      (2) Social Action Mirage (page 81)
      (3) Christian Education Mirage (page 82)
      (4) The Personal Responsibility Mirage (page 83)
      (5) The Goal-Setting Mirage (page 83)
      (6) The Pastor's Personal Interest Mirage (page 84)
   B. Which mirages do you think our congregation is most in danger of following?
   C. How do these mirages relate to the three golden threads of church growth?

3. Other Roadblocks (chapter 14, pages 85-90)
   A. Discuss these roadblocks to church growth. See if your class members can give at least one concrete illustration of each roadblock from their own experience:
      (1) The Pendulum Syndrome Block (page 85)
      (2) The Mission-Nuture Dichotomy Block (page 86)
      (3) The Anti-Manipulation Block (page 86)
      (4) The Denomination Block (page 87)
      (5) The Analysis Paralysis Block (page 87)
      (6) The Hard Work Block (page 88)
      (7) The Inactive Member Block (page 88)
      (8) The Numbers Game Block (page 89)
   B. In what ways and to what degree is our congregation's growth blocked?

SESSION 7. Part VI—Getting Started (pages 91-110)
   1. From the Inside Out (chapter 15, pages 91-94)
      A. Miller says that "dreams are the stuff that success is made from." (page 92) What are your dreams and goals for this congregation? List them on newsprint.
      B. For your class?
      C. For your own personal life?
   2. From the Outside In (chapter 16, pages 95-110)
      A. Describe and evaluate our past "success" in evangelism and church growth.
      B. What are you personally willing to do each week to respond to Christ's call to "go into all the world" and make disciples? (Mark 16:15)